1-5-76

DICK ROBERTS
CAPITALISM IN CRISIS

PATHFINDER PRESS, INC., NEW YORK

First edition, 1975

Copyright © 1975 by Pathfinder Press, Inc.
All rights reserved

Library of Congress Catalog Card No. 75-16886
ISBN: 0-87348-408-8 (cloth); 0-87348-409-6 (paper)
Manufactured in the United States of America

Pathfinder Press, Inc.
410 West Street
New York, N. Y. 10014

1895788

Contents

Preface

"Karl Marx pronounced his sentence of doom on capitalism in 1867; the system was diagnosed as the victim of an incurable disease, and although no timetable was given, it was presumed to be close enough to its final death struggle. . . .

"But the system did not die. On the contrary, it seemed to emerge from each attack of weakness with renewed strength and to rebound from each crisis with a vigor that dismayed the critics."

So wrote Robert Heilbroner in *The Worldly Philosophers* (1953). His book has been reprinted fifteen times, is standard diet in freshman college courses, and has been listed among the ten favorite books of corporate executives.

The complacency of American academics towards Marxism expressed by Heilbroner in the early 1950s no longer carries such conviction. Years of agony in Vietnam have demonstrated to all serious thinkers that if the American capitalist system is not in its "final" death agony, it is nevertheless in dire straits, the roots of which had been explained by Marxists. Economic crisis stalks the country and threatens the capitalist world. Domestic unemployment heads toward the levels of the Great Depression. Abroad, the scourge of famine sweeps Africa and Asia.

But Washington has no meaningful answers to these problems. It does not provide jobs for unemployed workers; it cannot provide decent education for all students regardless of color; it does not provide adequate medical care for its citizens and sufficient incomes for the aged. Washington's aggressive foreign policies are increasingly rejected by public opinion. The legitimacy of the government is more and more undermined in the eyes of working people. There is a new openness to new ideas—including the most radical.

Speaking on campuses across the country, I have found that, since the almost simultaneous eruption of Watergate and the energy crisis, there has been a far-reaching interest in the enormous economic problems facing capitalism and in the Marxist analysis of them.

The present book seeks to provide answers to many of the questions on the minds of working people and students: the causes of inflation and recession, the roots of and responsibility for high energy prices, the similarities and differences between the Great Depression and the world economic crisis today.

Capitalism does have an incurable disease: the private-profit drive of monopoly. Beginning with the opening study of the depression of the 1930s, I seek to show that the foreign and domestic policies of the U.S. government have been primarily dictated by the needs of the monopolists.

From this flows an aggravated contradiction in capitalist society which *is* fundamentally irreconcilable—the conflict between the powers and privileges of the capitalist ruling class that Washington protects, and the needs of workers, who are the overwhelming majority of the population, that the government cannot satisfy.

Close attention is given to the countercyclical economic policies advanced by John Maynard Keynes and increasingly adopted by Washington's economic experts in the post-World War II period. The inflationary epidemic they encouraged is traced to its roots in government deficits for war production.

Marxist theory has a continuity that predates the publication of Marx's *Capital* over a century ago. As early as the *Communist Manifesto* of 1848 Marx and Engels declared that capitalism inevitably led to economic crises, wars, and revolutionary upheavals. After these two pioneers, the most prominent exponents and practitioners of Marxism were the two central leaders of the Russian Revolution of October 1917—V.I. Lenin and Leon Trotsky. The analysis of modern capitalism first undertaken by these leading Bolsheviks, especially at the first four congresses of the Communist International and in Lenin's *Imperialism: The Highest Stage of Capitalism,* forms the basis of the theory applied in this book.

But it is a theory that has been continuously updated and enriched by the analysis of later events. Marxism has been most consistently carried forward, both as a tradition and as a living method of interpretation and political action, by the Fourth

International—the world party of socialist revolution founded by Trotsky in 1938.

Americans are forbidden to join this organization by the reactionary Voorhis law passed during the Second World War. But we are not forbidden to read its ideas and use them in analyzing American problems. The most recent comprehensive examination of the international recession of world capitalism, adopted by the Fourth International in 1975, is presented in the appendix.

From theoretical analysis and the lessons of practical experience, the revolutionary movement develops a program that can achieve victories for working people and the oppressed in their day-to-day struggles, and ultimately guide them toward abolishing the outmoded capitalist system. How can the gap between the immediate demands of exploited people and the objective possibility (and necessity) for socialism be bridged?

The answer to this crucial question boils down to finding concrete ways to mobilize the workers and their allies in mass actions around demands and proposals that correspond to the present needs and consciousness of millions of people—and at the same time systematically lead to a socialist revolution in which the workers take complete economic and political control of society. The "Bill of Rights for Working People," the 1976 election platform of the Socialist Workers Party, outlines such a set of proposals, fitted to the immediate problems and needs of American working people as the economic crisis of the 1970s deepens. It has also been included in the appendix.

Three of the essays in this book were published as separate articles between October 1974 and February 1975. They have been re-edited for this volume.

Dick Roberts
May 1975

The Last Great Depression and the Coming Crisis

The capitalist world has plunged into the first international recession since the 1930s. Although unemployment is much worse in the United States than in the other major capitalist nations, there is no leading capitalist country where the ranks of the unemployed are not growing and where industrial production is not slowing down.

On top of this, the inflation rate has never been higher in the capitalist world as a whole. Inflation in France, Britain, Italy, and Japan exceeded even the annual rate of over 12 percent that the United States suffered in 1974.

Moreover, there is a danger that the deepening U.S. recession and the inflationary expansion of credit could combine to throw the capitalist world into an economic crisis on the scale of 1929–32. After decades of claiming that the 1930s "can never happen again," today a number of experts believe that precisely this possibility faces world capitalism.

A case in point was an article in the July 28, 1974, *New York Times Magazine* by the newspaper's monetary expert, Leonard Silk. As a former editor of *Business Week* magazine and associate of the Brookings Institution, Silk is heeded in high places. Within a few weeks several Congressmen had entered his article into the *Congressional Record*.

"Today," Silk wrote, "the world economy is again threatened with breakdown and disintegration. Monetary disorder afflicts the entire non-Communist world. Nations coming up against the interlocked threats of trade and payments deficits, inflation, energy shortages and unemployment are growing increasingly nationalistic in their policies. It was beggar-my-neighbor nationalism that brought on the debacle last time, for in the end the nationalism turned demonic and aggressive in Germany and Japan. Such an outcome seems unthinkable today as it did in 1931."

Silk's central thesis, as his opening paragraph suggests, is that nationalism must give way to internationalism or another catastrophe cannot be avoided. He concludes, "The United States cannot dictate to the others; it does not have the power to do so, and it would only defeat its own purposes if it tried. What is needed now is genuinely shared leadership and the forging of a spirit comparable to that achieved in wartime—and to the reconstruction of the world after the last war."

A similar thesis is urged by Charles P. Kindleberger, international economic affairs specialist at the Massachusetts Institute of Technology. Professor Kindleberger's *The World in Depression, 1929-1939* brings to bear the findings of contemporary American academic monetary and fiscal theory to analyze the causes of the Great Depression. His central theme is that "part of the reason for the length, and most of the explanation for the depth of the world depression, was the inability of the British to continue their role of underwriter to the system and the reluctance of the United States to take it on until 1936" (p. 28).

Noteworthy here is the shift of attention away from the specific forms of governmental antirecessionary intervention to the more fundamental question of *capitalist nationalism versus internationalism*. Kindleberger considers himself a "realist" in economic disputations. It is not without significance that such representatives of the bourgeois economic establishment are returning now to study the actual evolution of the depression of the 1930s in the light of the failure of Keynesian regulators today to stem the world inflationary binge. By shifting the discussion to the much more fundamental level of capitalist foreign policy, Kindleberger in effect admits that domestic financial manipulations are not the cure-all they were once cracked up to be. He recognizes that no matter how sophisticated the Keynesian mechanisms became in the postwar period, they cannot stave off a new world crisis if they are applied only from the standpoint of national self-interest.

Throughout his description of the depression of the 1930s Kindleberger implies, and in brief concluding remarks he suggests, that only the assumption of "world leadership" by either the United States or the European Common Market can head off a new world collapse.

America in the Seventies

Apart from appeals to the enlightened self-interest of international capitalism to display a spirit of cooperation and compromise, a second theme that dominates the current writings of the professional economists is the readiness of the government to act disinterestedly on behalf of all the people of the nation if the worst should come to pass and a new economic collapse engulfs the world of the 1970s. The point of this, of course, is to sustain public trust in the system and discourage working people from advancing their own independent organizations, demands, and solutions. As evidence for this complacent view we are usually presented with a sanitized version of the history of Roosevelt's New Deal. Before taking up this historical case, it would not be out of place to pose a question for these defenders of the status quo. What leads them to believe that a society ruled by the pampered rich, contemptuous of working people in "normal" times, will act differently in an economic crisis?

Two vivid glimpses of capitalist America, one at the top, the other at the bottom of the heap, tell more about the gulf that separates the rulers from the ruled than a volume of statistical charts.

In June 1974 Alden Whitman—who usually writes obituaries for the *New York Times*—visited Newport, Rhode Island, and turned in an article on the wealthy people who spend the summer there. "Inflation?" Whitman asked. "For the 250 or so super-rich American families summering in their enclave here, it is but a distant happening like summer lightning. . . ."

These people have huge mansions in Newport, although they're only summer places. "The homes—some have seven or eight master bedrooms—are lived in only two or three months of the year, yet the furnishings—the rugs, the chairs, the tables, the china, the objets d'art—are all of top quality. . . .

"Every family has a cook—some have two—and maids and housemen and, sometimes, gardeners and butlers."

Mrs. John Drexel III complained to Whitman, "Every night it's a different dinner party. . . . It just exhausts me to look at my calendar."

Whitman suggested that "one explanation for inflation's featherlike touch here"—he delicately avoided saying it was *the* explanation—"is the vastness of the inherited fortunes." As one Newport upper crustacean remarked, "When your spendable income is a million bucks a year inflation stings a little, but it doesn't really hurt," although he added ruefully, "it's not the wad my grandfather had" (which is probably true, since as a tax dodge many of America's rulers have cut their "income" by stashing their money in various trust funds, foundations, and the like).

Whitman gave an example of the kinds of problems the Newport people face: "Jane Pickens Langley, whose late husband, William, was an investment broker, lives in a splendid old house on Bellevue Avenue. She has a personal maid who doubles as a hairdresser, but she is also troubled about help. 'I don't see why more people don't become domestics,' she said. 'It's such a lovely way of life, such a nice life. I let my servants have telephone calls and things of that type.'"

Of course the reality for tens of millions of Americans, the vast majority of whom are working people, not the owners of corporations, is that inflation has been cutting into living standards more and more, seemingly without end. And jobs are harder and harder to come by.

Much more indicative of the trend in the economy was another article, in the July 24, 1974, *New York Times,* which reported that the gap between Black and white Americans is continuing to widen. The Census Bureau reported that "the remarkable economic gains made by blacks during the nineteen-sixties slowed down, and in some cases were reversed, in the early nineteen-seventies."

This report showed that the median income for a Black family of two adults and two children in 1973 was $7,269, which everyone knows is not enough to live on in these inflationary times. The white family median income was $12,595, which isn't going to buy a house in Newport either.

According to the Census Bureau, about 5.1 million Blacks live in low-income sections of the twenty-six largest cities. This means that for every ruling-class family summering in Newport, there are 20,000 Blacks living in poverty in the big city ghettoes.

At the bottom of the American social ladder, which is supposed to be so easy to climb, are Black women workers. Still another article from the *New York Times* described the work of Mrs.

Annie McLaurin, who works in Forest, Mississippi, in a poultry factory. "She splits chicken gizzards. Every working day for six years she has stood beside a moving chain in a poultry processing plant and cut gizzards open with a pair of scissors.

"That is all. She never cuts the liver, or pulls out the craw, or picks out the pinfeathers or cuts the throat to spill the living blood.

"She does not even clean the gizzard. She merely cuts it open and passes it on. Some days she splits more than 4,000 gizzards."

Mrs. McLaurin told the *Times* reporter that the scissors are so dull that she can hardly cut, that her hands get sore and that some people cut off the ends of their thumbs. She is paid $2.10 an hour. She gets no vacation, no paid holidays, no sick leave, and no hospital insurance.

This was in 1974, more than forty years after the depression and after the government was supposed to have stepped in and ironed out the deficiencies in the capitalist system which brought that depression about. Millions of Americans lived in poverty in the best of times—and today it is clear that conditions are worsening drastically.

It is still too early to predict the precise forms that the deepening economic crisis here and abroad will take. But there is a critical fallacy in the reasoning of those, like Kindleberger, who put their faith in a sudden conversion of the rulers of America to capitalist internationalism. They believe that the last great crisis of world capitalism was the product of a series of mistakes. In essence, Kindleberger argues that the United States could have led world capitalism out of the crisis if the right decisions had been made.

But a study of the depression forces the opposite conclusion. The depression and the world war that followed underlined the inability of capitalist governments to follow any other policies than those in the immediate interest of their own ruling classes. And this was no less true of the "New Deal" itself. The very policy that is today so much remembered as a model of government intervention in behalf of the people, in reality clearly expressed stepped-up intervention by the government in defense of monopoly rule—against its capitalist competitors abroad and its working-class challengers at home.

For these reasons a review of the Great Depression contains lessons of the utmost importance, as the warnings of new crisis gather on the horizon.

The Stock Crash

On October 25, 1929, the *New York Times* carried the following report:

> The most disastrous decline in the biggest and broadest stock market of history rocked the financial district yesterday. In the very midst of the collapse five of the country's most influential bankers hurried to the office of J.P. Morgan & Co., and after a brief conference gave out word that they believed the foundations of the market to be sound, that the market smash has been caused by technical rather than fundamental considerations, and that many sound stocks are selling too low.

That was like the U.S.-is-winning-the-war-in-Vietnam reports by General Westmoreland that also got printed on the front page of the *New York Times.* Four days later the bottom fell out of the market. This triggered a general economic collapse. In *The Great Depression,* historian David A. Shannon writes:

> Within only a few months unemployment became a serious problem. Forlorn, down-and-out men shuffled hopelessly through bread lines. Banks began to fail at an alarming rate. Farm prices dropped to disastrous lows. City after city became unable to cope with its relief problems.
>
> The most disheartening aspect of the early depression was that there was no sign of a recovery. Earlier depressions had spent their force in a few months, the direction of the economy had reversed itself, and there had been a slow climb back to normal conditions. But in the Great Depression things became steadily worse for three and one-half years. [pp. ix–x]

For most people under fifty today the depression is a remote abstraction that has already passed into history. But for the tens of millions who lived through it, it was a time of blasted lives and desperate struggle for mere survival. Year after year unemployment remained above 10 million. Bread lines and inadequate skid-row-type relief kitchens were all that stood between mass hunger and outright starvation. Those who were poor to begin with were threatened with actual destruction as whole agricultural regions ceased production and farmers hit the road in the vain hope of finding distant fields untouched by the economic blight. (Their trials are chronicled for posterity in John Steinbeck's memorable *Grapes of Wrath.*)

In the relief agencies the appeals for help filled miles of filing cabinets. The faceless bureaucracy shuffled papers, granting or rejecting requests according to rules as mysterious as those of the temple priests of Delphi. The impersonal dossiers are eloquent even in the crabbed jargon of the government clerks. The Coreys, an Irish immigrant family living in New York City, applied for relief in 1933, the worst year of the depression; the clerk recorded:

Education
Man: Graduate, Catholic High School—Ireland.
Wife: Elementary school—Ireland.

Medical status
Man: Negative.
Wife: Very thin, looks undernourished.

Woman's Work History
Domestic from age of 14 in Ireland. In U.S.A., department store packer, factory worker until marriage. . . .

Number of Children in the Home
Seven; Ages—5 months to 8 years. . . .

First Application: . . . Man is a bill-poster, employed by an outdoor advertising company since 1928. Since September, 1932, he has had only two or three days work a week at $5 a day and, during the past three months, only a few days all told. Last week he worked only one day, and the week before, only six hours. Friends have helped with food. The couple and their . . . children live in two furnished rooms at $6 a week. They have moved four times in the last year. The children were described as robust and healthy and, according to the investigator, "home very untidy and ill-kept. Furniture old and battered. Evidence of poverty but no suffering."

Case Rejected because part-time earnings exceeded the deficit that would have permitted Home Relief supplementation. [cited by Shannon, pp. 155-56]

The great American dream!
The depression caught almost all people completely by surprise. The late 1920s had seen a boom—not for everyone, but nevertheless a boom. Hoover was elected in a landslide in 1928, declaring in his campaign that, "we in America are nearer to the final triumph over poverty than ever before in the history of any land."

John J. Raskob, the millionaire chairman of the Democratic Party National Committee and close associate of the mighty DuPont family of Delaware, said in the summer of 1929: "If a man saves $15 a week, and invests in good common stocks, and allows the dividends and rights to accumulate, at the end of twenty years he will have at least $80,000 and an income from investments of around $400 a month. He will be rich. And because income can do that, I am firm in my belief that anyone not only can be rich, but ought to be rich."

Both the Democratic and Republican prophets forgot, in the first place, the inevitability of downturns as well as booms in the capitalist business cycle.

The Business Cycle and Unemployment

Periodically the point is reached in every upturn where more goods have been produced than can be sold, and production has to be cut back.

Employment enters this business cycle as both a cause and an effect. While the economy is expanding, many additional workers are hired. But capitalism cannot tolerate full or even nearly full employment for any length of time, because workers take advantage of the demand for labor to push for a larger share of the value they produce. In the face of declining profit rates, and in order to weaken the unions and undercut wage demands, the capitalists will begin curtailing investment and encouraging a certain amount of unemployment. But as workers are laid off, the decline in their purchasing power eats into other sectors of the economy. Production falls even further, more workers lose their jobs, and the economy slumps.

The ebb and flow of workers into the plants is well illustrated in the American auto industry. At peak production, as many as 850,000 auto workers might be hired. But at the bottom this can fall to as low as 450,000, meaning that hundreds of thousands of workers have been pushed out of the plants in the process.

The most recent peak in auto production occurred in 1973. Today it is off 20 percent and still falling. New layoffs are announced every week.

When more and more workers are unemployed there is a tendency of those who do have the remaining jobs either not to risk fighting for wage increases or to make smaller demands than in the past for fear of being laid off. Workers who are unemployed are willing to work for less. The existence of this reserve army of labor—the ranks of the unemployed—pits workers against one another, creating a general downward pressure on wages.

In a racist and sexist society, the business cycle serves to keep the most oppressed—national minorities, women—in a state of permanent job instability. They are, indeed, the last hired and first fired. If a business upturn isn't long and strong enough, they may not get jobs at all. This is undoubtedly why the median income levels between Blacks and whites continued to widen even during the 1971-72 economic upturn. That upturn lasted less than two years. The unemployment level only got below 5 percent for a few months.

Bourgeois economists often attempt to deny that there are inherent causes in capitalism for the business cycle. They attempt to pin each recession on conjunctural factors. Nevertheless, business cycles have occurred regularly without exception since the birth of modern capitalism in the industrial revolution of the nineteenth century. The recession that began in the United States in 1974 is the sixth since World War II.

The First World War

But these business cycles also take place within longer historical epochs, the character of which is crucial to understanding the depression of the 1930s as well as the economic crisis unfolding today. For capitalism is a *world system,* and it is international developments above all that determine the basic character of the epoch.

The late nineteenth century saw a rapid expansion of world capitalism, based on the plundering of the colonial world by British and French imperialism—with the United States opening its own guns on the Caribbean and the Pacific beginning in 1898. This direct territorial aggrandizement led, as Lenin explained in his 1916 pamphlet *Imperialism,* to a division of world markets between the imperialist powers.

There were those who thought that the formation of international cartels, uniting the most powerful monopoly corporations of many countries, would lead to peace. They envisioned an "ultraimperialist" stage in which the aggressive nationalism of competing imperialist powers would be supplanted by international agreements on the respective shares of markets to be parceled out to each of the competing powers.

But this argument overlooks the *necessity of capital to expand.* Just as on a national scale competing capitals expand to the point where one or a few firms dominate each industry (Ford, Chrysler, GM in auto; IBM in computers, etc.), so the same monopolies must expand on an international scale as they inevitably saturate national markets. The monopolists have long known that an economic slump in a particular industry in one country, or even a general downturn in that nation, can be cushioned if goods can be exported and sold abroad.

Moreover, a monopoly is able to extract high prices from consumers by holding down production to make sure its product is in short supply. But this means that monopoly superprofits are created which cannot be invested in the given sector. This "surplus capital" must be invested elsewhere. Capital flows from one sector to the next and from one country to the next. There is a rapacious struggle for world markets between the most powerful multinational trusts.

The terrible onslaught of World War I began the crucial shift of world economic power from Europe to the United States. In *The Age of Imperialism* Harry Magdoff cites an evaluation of U.S. financial prospects in the First World War by Thomas W. Lamont, the most articulate member of the firm of J.P. Morgan & Co. We have already met Lamont, for he was one of the five bankers who on October 25, 1929, told Americans that there were lots of good buys on the stock market. Fourteen years earlier, in an article in the July 1915 *Annals* of the American Academy of Political and Social Science, Lamont

identified the elements of the change brought about by the first year of the war and which could become increasingly important, depending on how long the war was to run: (1) 'Many of our manufacturers and merchants have been doing wonderful business in articles relating to the war'; (2) the increase in war business contributed to a 'prodigious export trade balance'; (3) the good export trade balance enabled buying back United States securities held by foreign investors; (4) the repurchase of these securities helped to eliminate the drain of foreign exchange that had been going to pay interest and dividends to foreigners; (5) the resulting transformation from debtor to creditor status enabled the United States to lend to foreign nations on a large scale, and thus to become a major recipient, rather than a payer, of interest and dividends. [pp. 81–82]

Lamont was forced to qualify this rosy picture for the future of American capitalism. If wartime trade had given the Wall Street bankers the boost they needed to become the financial kingpins of the world, the end of the war would mean a reduction in U.S. military exports. The position of financial superiority could not be long defended if it was not based on solid exports of goods as well as money. As Lamont put it:

Many people seem to believe that New York is to supersede London as the money center of the world. In order to become the money center we must of course become the trade center of the world. . . . My guess would be that, although subsequent to the war this country is bound to be more important financially than ever before, it will be many years before America, even with her wonderful resources, energy, and success, will become the financial center of the world. Such a shifting cannot be brought about quickly, for of course to become the money center of the world, we must, as I have said, become the trade center; and up to date our exports to regions other than Great Britain and Europe have been comparatively limited in amount. We must cultivate and build up new markets for our manufacturers and merchants and all that is a matter of time. [p. 82]

While World War I began the shift of financial power to New York, the shift was not yet decisive. The struggle for markets would be intensified. Interimperialist rivalries would be escalated. The depression and even World War II itself were rooted in the inconclusive outcome of World War I.

This line of development was anticipated in a speech by Leon Trotsky entitled "The Premises for the Proletarian Revolution," which was published in *Izvestia,* August 5, 1924. Trotsky summarized the powerful but not yet dominant position of U.S. imperialism:

The United States produces one-fourth of the world grain crop; more than one-third of the oats; approximately three-fourths of the world corn crop; one-half of the world coal output; about one-half of the world's iron ore; about 60 percent of its pig iron; 60 percent of the steel; 60 percent of the copper; 47 percent of the zinc. American railways constitute 36 percent of the world railway network; its merchant marine, virtually nonexistent prior to the war, now comprises more than 25 percent of the world tonnage; and, finally, the number of automobiles operating in the trans-Atlantic republic amounts to 84.4 percent of the world total! While in the production of gold the United States occupies a relatively modest place (14 percent), thanks to its favorable trade balance, 44.2 percent of the world's gold reserve has collected in its vaults. The national income of the United States is two and a half times greater than the combined national incomes of England, France, Germany and Japan. These figures decide everything. They will cut a road for themselves on land, on sea and in the air. [*Europe and America,* p. 25]

Trotsky added that if the United States carried out its designs to "put Europe on rations," especially through demanding the repayment of war debts, the economic crisis would deepen and the march toward a new world war would be hastened. This is precisely what happened.

War Debts

Washington demanded repayment of the funds lent to its allies in the war; in order to finance these debts, Britain and France demanded payment of reparations by Germany. This vicious circle saw France's occupation of the Ruhr in 1923 and the eruption in Germäny of one of the worst inflations in history. Brian Johnson described it in *The Politics of Money:*

> Government expenditures, which had exceeded revenue by three to one in the years 1921-22, rose to ten to one in January 1923 as the government printed money to buy food for Ruhr workers who were passively resisting foreign occupation. By the autumn of 1923 . . . the Reichsbank could no longer keep up with the sheer physical task of printing sufficient currency. One hundred and thirty-three additional printing firms using 1,783 machines were needed to meet the demand, while more than thirty paper manufacturers worked round the clock to provide the paper for banknotes. [p. 64]

The Dawes Plan of 1924, named after the American vice-president who helped to negotiate it, continued to insist upon German payment of reparations but at the same time advanced a massive loan to Germany, literally putting the whole of German real estate up as collateral.

But now American capital, first of all buying up the Dawes Plan notes, was encouraged to invest in Germany, and soon billions of U.S. investment dollars were pouring into other European countries as well. American bankers were, after 1924, as anxious to float loans in Europe (with whole European industries offered as collateral) as a few years earlier they had been anxious to avoid risky European ventures.

The ebb and flow of U.S. investments in Europe has played an increasingly important role in the world economy of the twentieth century. In the period 1924-28, U.S. investments abroad helped spur the recovery of the late 1920s. But when the American stock market started booming in 1928-29 capital began to flow the other way—and not individual savings of $15 per week either!—while in the depression U.S. credit for Europe dried up almost entirely. This was one of the major factors making the depression so long and so deep on a world scale.

So far as war debts and reparations are concerned, Kindleberger emphasizes: "Reparations may not have been directly responsible for the depression . . . but together with war debts they complicated and corrupted the international economy at every stage of the 1920s and during the depression through to 15 June 1933" (p. 39). On that date, in the midst of world crisis, international bankers agreed to suspend reparations. The United States had demanded continued payment of war debts up to the "Hoover Moratorium" in 1931 when America was already deep in depression. Even by this time it was too late.

The American Boom

The boom of the U.S. economy in the twenties is perhaps most worth recalling for the fact that the "golden twenties" were not golden for workers. The decade opened with vicious antilabor repression. Many sections of the working class, such as the Massachusetts textile workers and the Kentucky miners, never shared in the upturn when it did take place.

For American farmers the 1920s were an uninterrupted decade of misery. The American market was glutted with agricultural produce. Net farm income, including that of prosperous dairy and truck farmers, fell from almost $9.5 billion in 1919 to $5.3 billion in 1928. When the depression came on top of this, the blight was horrendous. There are the famous photographs by Dorothea Lange and Walker Evans to remind us of the stark toll that producing too many goods under capitalism can take.

When the euphoria collapsed under the impact of the stock crash, investment began to be cut back almost immediately and the unemployed lines began to grow. Nevertheless the market collapse was not the underlying cause of the depression. The stock market registers the purchase and sale of securities, as investors—and the market is mainly dominated by large financial investors, not small holders—gamble on the upward and downward movements of the economy. But it is these movements of the economy that govern stock prices in the last analysis, not vice versa.

Recession became inevitable in the late 1920s as *normal* cyclical overproduction developed, fueled by the "automobilization of America" and the glut in the agricultural sector. The market crash sped up the crisis. Investment dropped precipitously. Investors who lost fortunes in the market foreclosed mortgages to raise cash, and construction rapidly dwindled. A parallel slide of construction (which is the largest U.S. industry) and auto production is guaranteed to send the American economy into recession, as it did in 1929 and as it is doing again in 1975.

Spotlight on Germany

But the depression cannot be explained by the failure of the American economy alone. Its deepest roots were in international trade and finance, in the continuation and intensification of interimperialist rivalry, and above all in the policies of the American banking system. As the depression deepened in the United States and as the U.S. cut its spending on the products of the rest of the world, in turn pulling them toward depression, New York refused to maintain the system with loans. To be sure, when business is contracting, when profit opportunities are rapidly shrinking, "normal" loans are out of the question. But the point had been reached by the end of 1930 where the sole possibility of retarding the slide lay in massive government-to-government loans. Only the United States was in a position to undertake such a rescue operation. But the citadel of world capitalism performed in normal capitalistic fashion. The loans were not made. Depression spread from the United States abroad.

Central in the world situation were the developments in Germany. In 1929 the Dawes Plan was replaced by the Young Plan. (Owen D. Young, an American financier, negotiated the plan with assistance from J.P. Morgan & Co.) New York continued to insist on repayment of the war loans to its allies, which in turn continued to exact reparations from Germany. The level of reparations was lowered somewhat, and a new loan to Germany was subscribed to by the major capitalist powers. But this time New York raised only $100 million; where the Dawes loan saw an enthusiastic oversubscription, the Young loan had to be discounted.

In order to meet its international obligations under the exacting terms demanded by foreign bankers, the German government undertook a drastic deflation. Revenues would be whipped out of the hides of German workers. "The deflationary policy was followed for two fateful years. . . ," Kindleberger writes. "In March 1930, 537,000 fewer were employed than in March 1929. . . . With Brüning's taking of office, the number rose to 1,432,000 in April and in August, after his first decrees, to two million. After Brüning's further deflationary steps of December 1930, the difference between March 1931 and March 1929 employment reached 2.8 million" (p. 139). The disastrous political consequences of these statistics in the triumph of Nazism are well known. But what were the roots of Germany's financial devastation?

At this time the rulers of Germany called for an end to reparations. Naval rearmament was begun. An Austro-German credit union was formed to protect these markets against foreign competition. France and the United States retaliated, further decreasing German credits.

When prices fall and profits decline, and along with them the prices of stocks, bank failures become inevitable. They erupted in smaller European banks in 1930, but it was the collapse of the biggest Austrian bank, the Credit-Anstalt, in mid-1931, that ushered in the chain-reaction closing of banks across the capitalist world. (The name "Credit-Anstalt" is being recalled in the financial press today because the summer of 1974 saw the closing of two major banks, the Franklin National Bank in the United States and I.D. Herstatt in Germany.)

The Credit-Anstalt difficulties spread to the banks of Hungary, Czechoslovakia, Rumania, Poland, and ultimately Germany. It was this financial chaos that finally produced the 1931 "Hoover Moratorium." But the generosity of American banks at this point was too little, too late. What was needed abroad was hard cash, not merely the agreement of New York bankers not to collect old debts.

When the financial crisis spread to Britain in September 1931, London went off the gold standard and the pound declined sharply, losing 25 percent of its value in a few days. This plunge had extraordinarily widespread impact because the British pound was the principal trading currency on the world market and banks everywhere held much of their reserves in pounds. The pound had suddenly been converted to a weapon of economic warfare for the British ruling class. The position of British exports was temporarily strengthened, but at the cost of slashing a quarter of the value from pounds held on deposit around the world and depriving the imperialist system of a stable currency.

Washington's refusal to back the dollar by gold in successive moves beginning in 1968, the two devaluations of the dollar in 1971–73, and the "free float" of international currencies today, have this as a historical precedent.

Protectionism

Side by side with the disastrous curtailing of credit, the competing capitalist countries increasingly adopted protectionist measures. The process was again given its biggest stimulus by the United States with the adoption in 1930 of the notorious Hawley-Smoot tariff law. Over one thousand American economists and thirty-four governments urged Hoover not to sign the bill, which slapped prohibitive tariffs on a wide variety of imports. But it had been overwhelmingly passed in both houses of Congress.

American capitalism invariably endeavored first and foremost to protect sales in its own domestic markets. This required reducing the flow of goods imported from abroad, whatever the effects were on the competing powers.

Retaliations began immediately and spread from country to country. Stymied by tariffs, uncertain because of floating currencies, and impeded by saturated world markets, world trade spiraled downwards.

But if there are no foreign outlets for exports, if investment abroad is restricted, then the safety valve for domestic overproduction is closed. The expansive needs of capital are thwarted. Business does not invest. Under these circumstances the American "downturn" of 1929 became a decade of unrelieved world depression.

Hoover

The "do-nothing" image of the Hoover administration has become such a staple of Democratic Party propaganda that it is worth noting that, on the contrary, the Republican White House attempted to extricate the economy from depression with many of the traditional means available to a capitalist government. Historians Dexter Perkins and Glyndon G. Van Deusen describe the palliative attempts. Hoover

> urged the railroad and utility executives . . . to continue and expand their construction activities; he instructed the government departments to speed up public works and recommended further appropriations by Congress; he assembled at the White House leading industrialists and urged them to maintain existing wage rates . . . he secured funds for expansion of the Federal employment service, and in the spring of 1930 he ordered a census of the unemployed; and he urged the Federal Farm Board to 'support a floor under prices of both wheat and cotton by loans and purchases.' [*The United States of America: A History*, p. 497]

The Federal Reserve Board adopted "easy money" policies. Interest rates were reduced month after month until, by May 1931, they stood at 1.5 percent—a far cry from the 12 percent level prevailing in money markets today. But when markets are declining, when there is no prospect of profits, exhortations by the president and even cheap money cannot make capitalists invest. Monetary theory dictated that the economy could be governed by manipulations of the money supply. But low interest rates did not increase the money supply when corporations refused to borrow money because they were disinclined to invest—a fact that was to greatly influence Keynes and the later development of countercyclical fiscal theory. Money began to contract in the United States, initially in the farm belt in Missouri, Indiana, Illinois, Iowa, Arkansas, and North Carolina, with the worst situation in Kentucky and Tennessee. By 1933, when Roosevelt took office, all the banks were closed across the land.

The New Deal

Central to any discussion of whether capitalism is capable of preventing, ameliorating, or halting a major depression is an examination of the policies of Roosevelt's first term. To what ends were the reforms undertaken? Did the New Deal actually succeed in putting the depressed American economy back on its feet?

There can be no question of the significance of the laws that were passed. In essence the New Deal represented the fact that the capitalist economy, left to its own devices, would collapse. Only state intervention to prop it up could keep capitalism working. At first sight, the list of steps undertaken is impressive:

The Emergency Banking Act of 1933 drastically increased the power of the executive over banks. The Federal Reserve Board was reorganized, giving its governors greater control of the credit system. The United States went off the gold standard. Now Britain and the United States were simultaneously using devalued currencies to bolster their positions in world trade.

Federal emergency relief apparatuses were set up to employ workers on a massive scale. According to Perkins and Van Deusen, "More than 180,000 activities were set in motion, and more than 4,000,000 people were given (at least temporarily) something to do in the grim winter of 1933-1934" (p. 522). At the time there were 12 to 14 million unemployed.

The Agricultural Adjustment Act of 1933 gave new impetus to government intervention in agriculture. Whatever its immediate effects, and these were not great, it marked a turning point in U.S. farm policies. Henceforth the government would subsidize agriculture by encouraging the curtailment of production, by limiting the acreage in given commodities, and by purchasing surpluses in order to support prices.

The National Industrial Recovery Act (known as the NRA) attempted, on paper, to reconcile industry and labor. On one side it granted big industry price-fixing privileges formerly denied by antitrust laws; on the other it granted labor the famous Section 7(a), supposedly guaranteeing the right of collective bargaining. When workers seized on this to help their struggle to build industrial unions, these were certainly not the results anticipated by White House lawyers. Massive strike struggles in San Francisco, Toledo, and Minneapolis erupted, paving the way for the building of the CIO.

The Tennessee Valley Authority granted a nominally public corporation the powers to develop the whole Tennessee Valley area and to undertake a wide conservation and development program.

The Emergency Relief Employment Act of 1935 replaced the temporary act of 1933–34. Now the government would undertake deficits on a more or less routine basis to finance public works programs for the unemployed. The Works Progress Administration functioned down to the opening of the Second World War.

Finally, and most important, there was the Social Security Act of 1935. Taxes would be levied on both employers and employees to support retired workers. This was undoubtedly the most important and perhaps the last great concession by the American ruling class to the care of workers, as minimal as it indeed is. (The notorious inability of older men and women to live on the fixed incomes dictated by Social Security in face of rampant inflation has become an important issue in this country today.)

Myth and Fact

There are two closely interrelated sides to the mythology of the New Deal: first, that it introduced extensive governmental planning into the capitalist system which can act as an effective antidote to economic crises; second, that in expanding the power of the capitalist government over social life the state was demonstrating its commitment to the welfare of the average citizen. This package was wrapped up and sold to the American people through a massive propaganda campaign focused on the manufactured charisma of Franklin Delano Roosevelt, supported by the trade-union bureaucracy and the Communist Party.

The myth that Roosevelt initiated the New Deal as a "friend of labor" and that the Democratic majority in Congress represented the interests of workers as it passed New Deal legislation obscures the real reason the reforms were undertaken. And this myth—that the Democratic Party is capable of gradually altering capitalism for the better—is one of the biggest obstacles to real social progress in the United States today.

The mystification on which the "labor-liberal coalition" is built is false on all counts. "New Deal" methods may have functioned during the long post–World War II boom, when American capitalism enjoyed unrivaled supremacy in the world market, but in the actual depression that they were meant to halt they proved to be a failure. Nor was this a preplanned program for the rationalization of capitalist anarchy as it is sometimes portrayed. It was a halting patchwork of laws whose economic-regulatory side was ineffective and whose social reforms were undertaken *only under mass pressure* in an unprecedented emergency.

Roosevelt did not succeed in restoring the economy to production or returning the world market to tranquility, feats that proved entirely beyond the capacity of Roosevelt and his class without the inferno of the Second World War. What he did accomplish was (1) to protect American capitalist rule at home by skillfully magnifying every social reform wrenched from the system by an angry working class and (2) to mobilize the economy for the war that would ultimately permit American imperialism to reap the benefits that had been brought within reach by the economic conquests of World War I.

Let's take a closer look at the reforms of the New Deal.

The 1933 bank moratorium in fact allowed the big banks to consolidate their assets while thousands of small ones never opened again or paid back only a fraction of deposits. Art Preis, in his invaluable history of the building of the CIO, quotes Raymond Moley, one of Roosevelt's closest associates in the early years of the New Deal: "It cannot be emphasized too strongly that the policies which vanquished the bank crisis were thoroughly conservative policies. If there ever was a moment when things hung in a balance, it was on March 5, 1933—when unorthodoxy would have drained the last remaining strength of the capitalist system. Capitalism was saved in eight days." And Preis adds: "The man who promised to drive the 'money changers from the Temple' actually gave them a new lease on it" (*Labor's Giant Step*, p. 10).

The relief programs of 1933–34 and 1935–36 and the WPA were

entirely inadequate to the actual needs of workers. Temporary jobs were never provided for more than 25 percent of the jobless.

"Relief jobs," says Preis, "were systematically increased before national elections and hundreds of thousands were fired shortly after the votes were counted. . . .

"Throughout the entire first two terms of the Roosevelt administration, there were continuous unemployed demonstrations, relief works strikes and riots. The highest relief, the most relief jobs and the biggest wages were in direct proportion to the amount of unemployed struggles" (p. 11). Preis should know. He was a leader of the unemployed leagues.

There were, in fact, only two years in the decade stretching from 1929 to 1939 that saw economic improvement in the United States—1936 and 1937. At its lowest point unemployment still stood above four and a half million. A new recession began in 1937 and on the eve of World War II there were ten million unemployed workers.

Let us return to the Corey family, the Irish immigrants who were refused relief in 1933. Six years later, in June 1939, their last entry in the relief records reads:

> In the investigator's opinion . . . the Coreys are a good, simple couple, who worry about their large family but continue to have children because they are deeply religious. . . . He knows that Mr. Corey helps his wife with all the work in the home and that he is more than willing to do anything in the way of a job. He is without skills, other than bill-posting, and there is little chance of his getting back into this work. . . .
>
> Investigator believes that there will have to be a really widespread upswing in business before an unskilled person such as Mr. Corey could be placed. . . . The investigator thinks that it would be good for Mr. Corey to be given a WPA job. . . . He thinks that Mr. Corey should be helped to achieve citizenship since this would make him eligible for WPA. In his opinion and that of the supervisor, private agencies should help these people become citizens. In this instance they think that the Catholic Charities should assume that responsibility. [cited by Shannon, pp. 158–59]

In good times U.S. monopoly has always opened its doors to cheap foreign labor—the bigger the boom, the larger the masses of poor and untrained workers from abroad who pour into the city slums searching for jobs at low wages. But in bad times they are the first fired. Moreover they are made the target of racist and chauvinist propaganda about how "immigrants steal jobs" as unemployment increases. The lies and threats directed against

Chicano and Latino workers today repeat what was said about the Japanese and other Asian workers before and during World War II, and the Irish and Italian workers in earlier crises.

It was not the New Deal relief that put workers back on the job. It was building weapons for the impending slaughter of World War II.

The New Deal's agricultural policies (actually initiated in the Hoover administration) relieved pressure on the American farmer to a certain extent. Ultimately, however, monopolization of agriculture would drive most small farmers out of business, and in the 1970s the price support system would give way before the reign of "agribusiness."

Nor were the farm policies of the 1930s granted from on high through sheer benevolence. In 1932, for example, the Farm Holiday Association staged a massive nineteen-state strike; roads were blocked to prevent goods from coming to market, foreclosures were forcibly resisted and purchasers at mortgage sales harassed.

And in the last analysis the farm price support system in the United States testifies not so much to the productive ability of capitalism as to its deeply irrational and anarchic character. "It will be recorded in history," Trotsky wrote in 1939,

> that the government of the most powerful capitalist country granted premiums to farmers for cutting down on their planting, i.e., for artificially diminishing the already falling national income. The results are self-evident: despite grandiose productive possibilities secured by experience and science, agrarian economy does not emerge from a putrescent crisis, while the number of the hungry, the preponderant majority of mankind, continues to increase faster than the human population of our planet. Conservatives consider it sensible politics to defend a social order which has descended to such destructive madness and they condemn the socialist fight against such madness as destructive Utopianism. [*Marxism in Our Time*, p. 26]

The NRA, which was ultimately sacked by the Supreme Court, was a hoax from beginning to end. Its central economic intent was to push what antitrust legislation did exist on the books out of the way in order to step up the centralization of power in the hands of big firms, including the open permission of monopoly price fixing. To get this across, NRA was cloaked in the phony concept of reconciling the interests of capital and wage labor. Section 7(a), in deliberately ambiguous language, gave as much of a green light to the formation of *company unions* as genuine labor unions. In fact more company unions were formed in the NRA period than real trade unions, and when, in increasingly massive strike struggles, workers attempted to build industrial unions, the Roosevelt administration stepped in as a brutal strikebreaker.

"What followed the signing of the NRA," Preis writes, "was not the recognition of labor's rights but the most ferocious assault on American labor in its history. Labor was forced into what was a virtual civil war fought on three thousand miles of picket lines for five years. Hundreds of workers were killed, thousands wounded, tens of thousands arrested or otherwise victimized from 1933 to 1938" (p. 17).

It is also important to remember that the ideas advanced by John Maynard Keynes about how to remedy the crisis were not actually adopted by the Roosevelt administration during the depression. According to Keynes, the government should undertake deficit spending in hard times to provide funds for production and jobs which the economy itself cannot provide. These deficits, that is, government expenditures over and above what the government takes in in taxes, would be raised by large-scale bank loans to the government. In good times the government would be able to repay the loans at interest and the banks would also profit from the enterprise.

But in the actual depression of the 1930s the deficits incurred by Washington fell far short of stimulating revival. The highest U.S. deficit during the entire depression was $4.4 billion in 1936. But in 1943, as the industrialists churned out weapons to defeat rival imperialists (and reap historic profits), the deficit was $57.4 billion. In the three war years 1943–45, Washington's deficits were more than five times as much as in the ten depression years 1931–40. It was the successful effects of pumping massive deficits into the economic bloodstream to buy war goods—not theory!— that persuaded Washington that Keynes had something to say.

Ironically, Keynes himself had written in his most famous work, at the bottom of the depression in 1935, that "wars have been the only form of large-scale loan expenditure which statesmen have thought justifiable" (*The General Theory of Employment, Interest, and Money,* p. 130).

Thus, despite the prevailing conception that the New Deal illustrated the ability of the capitalist government to undertake economic reforms and to salvage the economy from crisis, it must be underlined that *World War II* put American capitalism back on its feet. Textbook historians Perkins and Van Deusen admit as much. "The New Deal did not bring about recovery. . . ." they write. "The fact is that new investment, on the average of about $9.5 billion during the years 1925 to 1929, averaged only $1 billion for the period 1933 to 1935, and only $2 billion for the relatively favorable period 1935 to 1939. The number of unemployed, about thirteen million when Roosevelt took office, shrank to a low of four and a half million in the summer of 1937, but in each winter it was about nine or ten million; by March, 1938, it had risen to eleven million, and it remained around ten million until March of 1939" (pp. 575–76).

Nevertheless, there is the attempt to embellish the Roosevelt administration with the conception that it achieved fundamental social reforms. Perkins and Van Deusen write that "in the years from 1933 to 1945 a deeply significant change in the economic balance of power in the United States took place: a diminution in the influence of the business classes, together with an enhancement of the role of the farmer, and, still more important, of labor" (p. 516). The assessment has little to do with reality.

Shaken by the stock crash of 1929 and the mass social discontent that erupted in the 1930s, the monopolists nevertheless used their power to check the people, and in the cases of millions, to force them to go hungry. Wealth was ever more tightly concentrated in the few biggest banking and industrial trusts, whose spread of investments beginning in the 1920s became the multinational world empire of U.S. imperialism following its bloody victory in World War II.

Ferdinand Lundberg, in *America's 60 Families,* published at the acme of the New Deal in 1937, documented the tight control of the ruling class over the mass media and the Democratic and Republican parties, in addition to their bases of power in the industrial corporations and banks.

Interestingly, in Alden Whitman's description of Newport high society, he mentioned five names that were on Lundberg's list of sixty in 1937: the Firestones, of the rubber trust; the Vanderbilts, of the New York Central Railroad; the Whitneys, the second most powerful family in Standard Oil; the Drexels, partners in the J.P. Morgan banking empire; and the Dukes, of the American Tobacco Company. Whitman was not writing about ruling-class families in the nineteenth century nor in the 1920s and '30s, but in 1974. They are the same families because their corporations had already become dominant in the first decades of this century. They have expanded even more since then because of the United

States victory in World War II and the global markets that opened up for U.S. investment.

Labor did take a giant step in the 1930s with the formation of the CIO. This was not a bounty of the New Deal but the fruit of sharp class battles against those whose interests it was designed to serve.

And only when private monopoly turned its eyes on war production and the prospects of world empire did the depression come to an end.

U.S. "Leadership"?

Monetary expert Kindleberger does not deny that the rearmament of the major capitalist powers pulled the world out of the depression. But he sidesteps the most important implications. "Whether United States leadership in rebuilding the world economy would have been forthcoming without the war is a question which cannot be answered," says Kindleberger. "A start had been made, but there was little follow-up." In the 1930s, "the world was far from the powerful leadership felt during and after the war in the provisions for rebuilding the world economy embodied in the Atlantic Charter, Article VII of Lend-Lease, Dumbarton Oaks, Bretton Woods, Hot Springs, the Anglo-American Financial Agreement, the International Trade Organization and General Agreement on Tariffs and Trade, the Marshall Plan and Point IV. Not only was American initiative feeble and hesitant; there was no alternative to it" (p. 290).

But this conception of "American leadership" is way off base. U.S. imperialism marched into World War II with its eyes solely on its own interests of global expansion. The wartime and postwar trade, financial, and political agreements listed by Kindleberger manifested not internationalism on Washington's part but the *dominance* of U.S. capitalism over its wartime allies as well as its defeated opponents in the postwar world. Lend-Lease aid hinged on the agreement of the recipient capitalist powers to open up their (and their colonies') markets to U.S. goods and capital. Bretton Woods placed international finance on the gold-exchange standard *backed by the dollar*. And in the Marshall Plan (and NATO) Washington simply recognized the imperative necessity of pouring money and armaments into the weakened European countries to protect them from internal revolution, thus protecting its own strategic interests and opening up new markets as well.

Following the war the United States exported goods and capital to Europe as never before. American multinational trusts grew on the foundations of the treaties Kindleberger holds up as models.

Is Washington, faced with intensified competition from the formerly subdued allies, now giving any evidence of providing a different kind of "leadership"? Kindleberger urges that the U.S. government's "exchange controls of 1963 to 1968 and the 1970–71 wave of protectionism" be "reversed." But this is not happening.

Nixon's "New Economic Policy" remains the order of the day under Ford. The dollar has been devalued a second time since Kindleberger wrote the above-quoted sentences and all the major world currencies are floating as a result. As the warning signs of economic crisis are ever more evident and alarming, the capitalist United States, as it did in the 1930s, places its highest priority on advancing its own position in world trade and finance to the detriment of its rivals and to the distress of poorer and weaker nations.

The obliviousness of the wealthy parasites summering in Newport symbolizes the essential blindness and callousness of America's ruling class at this juncture. The richest and most powerful nation has not succeeded in bringing out of poverty many millions of people in this country, let alone made any meaningful effort whatsoever to aid the hundreds of millions starving elsewhere in the capitalist world. The anarchy of the capitalist system cannot be brought under control by a capitalist government because, in the crunch, the ruling class always defends itself first of all. This important lesson of the 1930s and World War II must not be forgotten as a new world crisis looms.

The Explosive Inflation
They Failed to Foresee

I

As the short boom of 1972-73 gives way to international recession, the central feature in the world economy is the highly inflationary character of the economic conjuncture—an inflation without historical precedent.

The twenty-four-nation Organization for Economic Cooperation and Development (OECD) declared after a meeting in Paris that as of May 1974 consumer prices were rising simultaneously in the major industrialized countries by more than 1 percent per month, for the sixth consecutive month.

Real wages are declining across the globe; in many underdeveloped countries with large populations, food shortages—exacerbated by spiraling feed grain and fertilizer prices—have reached crisis proportions.

A new tone of concern has been appearing in the press. *Business Week* magazine, one of the soberer voices of New York finance, published a special issue on the crisis of the world capitalist economy July 6, 1974. It warned of "social unrest" abroad.

"Plainly . . . every country faces a time limit," said *Business Week*. "Inflation must be brought under control fairly quickly or the very fabric of European society will begin to unravel. The signs of strain are most visible in Italy where still another governmental failure could bring the Communists closer to power than they have come in any Western European government. The worry in France is that workers and students will stage a repetition of their 1968 uprising."

When it comes to the question of *explaining* the world inflationary crisis, the bourgeois press expresses bewilderment. *Business Week* complained June 29, 1974: "Economists will remember 1974 for many things: for the squeeze on energy, for the breathtaking rise in prices, and perhaps for events yet to come. But mainly they will remember 1974 as the year the forecasters blew it."

For without exception, the major financial newspapers, and the corporate and academic sources they draw upon, "failed utterly to foresee the explosive inflation"—in other words, they missed the most important economic fact about 1974.

The prevailing tone in the capitalist press is that the "inflation came out of nowhere," that its causes are "too complex," that another depression is possible and even unavoidable.

"Kondratieff Cycles"?

An article with an extreme viewpoint that received widespread commentary appeared in the June 27, 1974, *New York Review of Books.*

British historian Geoffrey Barraclough believes that "The Coming Depression" is an inevitable result of long-term cycles in the capitalist economy. "We stand at the end of an era, of a fifty-year period of history, of the age of neocapitalism. We are entering a period of radical readjustment, which is bound, before it ends, to breed misery and widespread suffering; it will be a traumatic experience, as long as it lasts. . . .

"What seems certain is that some solution to the problem of uncontrolled inflation will have to be found, if the fabric of society is not to be torn apart. . . ."

In order to explain the cataclysm and, in effect, to remove it from its actual causes in the capitalist world, Barraclough revives the theories of the Russian economist Nikolai Kondratieff. Kondratieff headed the Business Research Institute in Moscow after the 1917 revolution until he was exiled to Siberia in 1930 by the Stalin regime.

Kondratieff believed that he had located a "fifty-year cycle" in the world economy which saw twenty-five-year periods of upturn and twenty-five-year periods of downturn. The shorter *business cycles* take place within Kondratieff's overall rising or falling frameworks. Kondratieff's three waves were as follows: First long wave, rising from the end of the 1780s or the 1790s until 1810–17 and declining until 1844–51. Second long wave, rising from 1844–51 until 1870–75 and declining until 1890–96. Third long wave, rising from 1890–96 until 1914–20. "The decline probably begins in the years 1914–20," Kondratieff said.

James B. Shuman and David Rosenau attempt to popularize this theory in *The Kondratieff Wave: The Future of America Until 1984 and Beyond,* and it is this book that drew Barraclough's attention to Kondratieff. Shuman and Rosenau appear to believe that a new wave began in World War II, rose until about 1970 and is now in its decline. They believe the wave to be somehow inherent in capitalism without root causes. They write, "There seems to be no rational basis for the upswing of the long wave any more than there is for the downswing." (See p. 76.)

Although Kondratieff did not make claims for his discovery beyond the empirical data, he tended to imbue the "long wave" with powers of its own. In a 1935 article, "The Long Waves in Economic Life," he wrote: "We believe ourselves justified in saying that the long waves, if existent at all, are a very important and essential factor in economic development, a factor the effects of which can be found in all the principal fields of social and economic life."

Barraclough writes:

1895788

> Kondratieff . . . forces us to view it [the current world situation] in historical perspective, not as the unhappy outcome of a series of historical accidents caused by a glut of foot-loose Eurodollars, the greed of Arab sheiks, the costs of the Vietnam war, or the machinations of overmighty multinational corporations (though all these and other things enter in), but rather as a particular phase in a recurrent phenomenon, which has its parallels in the past. . . .
>
> Finally, if we accept the Kondratieff cycle, it conveys the frightening warning that we are only at the beginning of the 'lean years' and that we must suppose that things will get worse before they get better.

Long-term rising and falling trends of the world capitalist economy are a matter of historical record. The late nineteenth and early twentieth centuries saw an explosive expansion of European and American capitalism based on world conquest— Britain and France in the Far East, Arab East, and Africa; America in the Caribbean and Pacific, etc. This "division of world markets," as Lenin emphasized, directly paved the way for World War I.

The First World War was followed by years of almost uninterrupted international economic crisis, within which the upswing of the 1920s shortly gave way to the world disaster of the 1930s. Only the rebuilding of the imperialist military machines for a new round of terrible slaughter, in order again to "redivide" world markets, revived the economies.

Unlike the aftermath of the First World War, the aftermath of the second saw a new long-term upswing of world capitalism. Above all, the United States, as the military and economic victor of the war, spread its investments internationally. The Bretton Woods monetary conference in 1944 based world trade and finance on the dollar. U.S. armies policed the underdeveloped world to make it safe for "democracy." Within this long-term expansion, the American boom of 1961 to 1969 was the biggest and longest in history.

The trouble with the Kondratieff-Barraclough explanation, however, is that it *removes* these long-term trends from history, by attributing the upswings and downswings to something inherent in the cycle rather than in the real world within which the cycle takes place. This approach, bordering on the metaphysical, was criticized by the Bolsheviks at the time (though they naturally did not punish Kondratieff as Stalin was later to do). In a 1923 article, "The Curve of Capitalist Development," Leon Trotsky wrote:

> The periodic recurrence of minor [business] cycles is conditioned by the internal dynamics of capitalist forces, and manifests itself always and everywhere once the market comes into existence. As regards the large segments of the capitalist curve of development (fifty years) which Professor Kondratieff incautiously proposes to designate also as cycles, their character and duration are determined not by the internal interplay of capitalist forces but by those external conditions through whose channel capitalist development flows. The acquisition by capitalism of new countries and continents, the discovery of new natural resources, and, in the wake of these, such major facts of 'superstructural' order as wars and revolutions, determine the character and the replacement of ascending, stagnating, or declining epochs of capitalist development.

Trotsky's criticism of Kondratieff indicates the question we should ask: What external conditions of world capitalism have brought about its stagnation in the 1970s?

World Competition

Barraclough would like to avoid this question. He recognizes that after World War II the U.S. government pursued policies aimed at expanding American business abroad, and that the decisions taken at the Bretton Woods conference were designed to advance this aim. But, says Barraclough, "considering the small part that foreign trade played (and still plays) in the United States economy, this obsession with foreign markets is easier to explain on psychological than on rational grounds."

To Barraclough, Dean Acheson, then an undersecretary of state, was merely "expressing a prevalent view" in 1944 when he declared: "You don't have a problem of production. The United States has unlimited creative energy. The important thing is markets. . . . My contention is that we cannot have full employment and prosperity in the United States without the foreign markets."

Barraclough's argument is frequently repeated: exports constitute only a small fraction of the Gross National Product (for a long time they hovered around 4 percent of GNP); consequently foreign markets are relatively unimportant.

This argument ignores the inherent necessity of capitalism to expand. As they became multinational corporations, for example, the Big Three U.S auto trusts—General Motors, Ford, and Chrysler, around which more than a tenth of the American economy swirls—swallowed up or drove into bankruptcy over 2,000 auto competitors. Today GM sells one-third of the motor vehicles produced in the capitalist world.

Is this an irrational quirk to be explained only by peculiar attributes of three generations of GM top management? On the contrary, it flows from the laws of capitalist competition. A corporation that does not continue to expand its markets, or at least to defend them from competitors who are expanding, goes under. Monopoly, and ultimately *multinational monopoly,* reflect the competitive pressures of an increasingly international capitalist market.

The GNP percentage argument overlooks three facts.

1. It overlooks the fact that a small percentage of GNP nevertheless can represent a large and crucial percentage of the markets of the individual industries actually involved. U.S. agricultural exports usually represent about 20 percent of total U.S. exports, and consequently they are less than 1 percent of the U.S. GNP. Nevertheless, figures for 1970 (the year is intentionally chosen to precede the U.S.-USSR wheat trade pact and the recent upsurge of U.S. agricultural exports) showed that the United States exported 39 percent of its wheat, 15 percent of its corn, 38 percent of its soybeans, and 71 percent of its rice.

Tell the New Orleans rice brokers that their preoccupation with foreign trade is "psychological"! Clearly these industries would go under without foreign markets. The preoccupation with foreign markets is (and has been for a century) an important determinant of U.S. foreign policy. It plays no small part in the cruel famine now affecting underdeveloped countries, as will be discussed in more detail below.

2. It overlooks the fact that the import-export trade, even when

it is a fraction of a given industry, is crucial in the determination of the prices and profits of that industry. Foreign automobiles account for less than 20 percent of the U.S. auto market, but it is competition with foreign auto producers that forces the Big Three to build smaller and cheaper cars.

Less known is the case of steel. For a number of years the U.S. steel industry called the shots in world steel production and pricing. Toward the latter half of the 1960s, however, the formation of giant steel trusts in Japan and Europe seriously eroded this position. *Business Week* magazine complained December 14, 1968:

> At least since World War II, purchasing agents have had a pretty easy time of it predicting price trends in steel: They were bound to be up. Certainly, the 1950s' bludgeon tactics of across-the-board boosts in steel prices faded in the 1960s. But the upward trend did not alter. Now, though, the old order is changing, and early last month, Bethlehem Steel Corp., the No. 2 producer, slashed hot-rolled carbon sheets by $25 a ton to "meet domestic competition."
>
> Steel executives couldn't recall a more drastic price cut since the rampant competition of the early 1930s, nor could they recall a more direct challenge to the industry's leader, U.S. Steel Corp.

The heightened U.S. competition was a direct product of heightened world competition and the world glut of steel markets.

3. By emphasizing exports of goods, it overlooks the equally crucial necessity of monopoly capitalism *to export capital.* For monopoly must restrict production in order to keep up prices. The resulting "surplus capital" must find markets.

Since World War II, U.S. industry has sent tens of billions of dollars abroad to build the foreign subsidiary corporations of U.S. multinationals. Many of the U.S. giants do more foreign business than they do domestic business. Exxon sells more oil in Europe than in the United States—and given the recent energy squeeze, it need hardly be added, at much greater monopoly profits. The overseas sales of U.S. corporations constitute a "Gross National Product" that is the third largest in the world after the United States and the Soviet Union!

Dean Acheson, not Professor Barraclough, accurately stated the needs and aspirations of U.S. imperialism for foreign markets.

Furthermore, it is precisely in the arena of international competition that we must locate the external conditions that force world capitalism into the *stagflationary*—inflationary *and* recessionary—crisis.

The markets that were opened up to U.S. (and foreign) capital and goods following World War II were not unlimited. The most significant factor was the rebuilding of Europe and Japan from the ashes of destruction. New plants incorporated the technological discoveries of the war years. Often this technology surpassed the obsolete facilities of the U.S. and Britain.

While the United States suffered frequent recessions following the war (it is now in its sixth postwar recession), for roughly fifteen years, into the mid-1960s, Europe and Japan sustained almost uninterrupted economic growth. These rising overseas economies cushioned the downturns in the United States.

When industries could not find sufficient markets in the United States, they could sell abroad. If there were insufficient investment outlets, the corporations "multinationalized" themselves. Subsidiary firms were built abroad, absorbing investments and at the same time carving out significant sections of foreign markets. Meanwhile the expansion of Europe and Japan depended heavily on the export of goods—European goods going mainly to other European nations within the Common Market, Japanese goods going mainly to the United States.

But this mutually reinforcing expansion began to run out of steam after the war-torn economies had been rebuilt.

A point was inevitably reached at which the rate of industrial expansion slowed down. Among the advanced capitalist countries, this was seen first in Europe and then in Japan.

"Europe's postwar economic boom that blended explosive growth, full employment, moderate inflation, and political stability is over," *Business Week* announced on July 6, 1974. "Most European economies have slowed sharply, but the rate of inflation keeps going higher. Unemployment is up all over Europe and there is hardly a stable government in sight. . . .

"Japan's 'economic miracle' has skidded to a grinding halt, the victim of the oil crisis and soaring raw materials prices. Confronted by the highest inflation rate of any major industrial country, slackening consumer demand, and the slowest GNP growth in two decades, the nation is at an agonizing turning point in its industrial—and social—development."

Business Week, of course, leaves out the key role that U.S. policies have played in deepening the world crisis and touching off the recent round of inflation that threatens to bring down businesses and banks, but so do commentators like Professor Barraclough.

U.S. Imperialist Offensive

President Nixon's declaration of a "New Economic Policy" on August 15, 1971, marked a "turning point within a turning point" of world capitalist development. The signs of stagnation and deepening crisis were already on the horizon.

In 1964-65 the British Labour Party, under Harold Wilson's leadership, imposed an "austerity" program on the workers, and by November 1967, the devaluation of the pound further signaled that the once mighty British imperialism would be among the first casualties of a new world capitalist crisis. Massive workers' struggles in France in 1968, in Italy since 1969, and on a broad scale in Britain since 1971, all reflected the stagnating standard of living in Europe, the beginning of the erosion of real wages, and the fact that the working class would not willingly accept the costs of a new round of capitalist contradictions.

In the United States real wages were essentially frozen beginning in 1965 under the impact of war-primed inflation. (They turned upward briefly in 1971-72, only to be hit all the harder by the food-price inflation that erupted in the spring of 1973.)

Within the context of increasingly saturated and inflationary national markets, world trade becomes even more critical. Multinational monopoly is forced to scan the globe for the "best buy" and the "highest-paying customer."

As inflation racked the United States in the late 1960s, billions of dollars' worth of foreign goods poured into the American market; higher-priced U.S. goods found it increasingly difficult to meet competition in foreign markets; the inflated dollar grew weaker and weaker, periodically upsetting the international monetary system. To add further injury to American capitalism, workers struck the mightiest of all U.S. industries in late 1970 and showed signs that the pattern set at General Motors might be repeated elsewhere in the land.

This was the background to Nixon's 1971 proclamation. In essence, his "New Economic Policy" signaled that U.S. imperialism would take the high road of trade and financial warfare on an international scale and, at home, use every instrument of the government to keep workers and wages in line. It is now possible to make initial estimates of the impact of Nixon's policy. For one thing, it is increasingly clear that the inflation sweeping world capitalism today is intimately connected to the sharp escalation of U.S. economic warfare initiated on August 15, 1971.

Oil

The world energy crisis most clearly disclosed the aggressive policies of U.S. corporations in the intensified struggle for markets. Whether the decision to raise oil prices in the winter of 1973 was initially made in New York or in the Arab East is a moot point. What is clear, however, is that Washington made no move to resist the rise of world oil prices and that U.S. imperialism benefited from this development.

The major oil corporations worked in concert with Arab regimes as the crisis deepened.

Higher oil prices became one of the main generators of spiraling world prices generally. From synthetic fabrics to fertilizer, a host of essential commodities directly require petroleum or petroleum by-products.

Some efforts have been made to present the United States as a country that will suffer along with everybody else because of higher oil-import prices. These, it is true, have been helpful to the oil trusts in driving up domestic gasoline and heating fuel prices. But so far as the ebb and flow of U.S. profits is concerned, U.S. capital has much to gain from the energy squeeze. The main factors were explained by Dewey Daane, a member of the board of governors of the Federal Reserve System, in testimony before a U.S. Senate subcommittee on May 30, 1973, *five months before* the October War and its consequences.

> It should be noted, first, that not all of the increase in U.S. payments for oil imports will constitute a net drain on the U.S. current account balance. There will be substantial offsets in the form of increased U.S. exports to those oil-producing countries that do have sizable populations and development needs. There will be further offsets in the form of increasing earnings by U.S. petroleum companies engaged in foreign operations, and a reduced need for U.S. financing of the future expansion of the industry.
>
> Second, those oil-exporting countries that do add very substantially to their foreign assets over the decade will be seeking secure and profitable investment outlets for these funds. It seems likely that a substantial portion will be invested in the United States. . . .
>
> Third, other industrial countries in Europe and Japan will also be increasing their oil imports. They are, and will remain, much more dependent than this country on rising oil imports. . . . [*The International Financial Crisis*, p. 19]

Nor will the nationalizations of the holdings of the oil trusts have a significant effect on profits. For these corporations still

control the world markets where oil is consumed. "Few informed
people dispute the oil industry's ability to survive and many even
predict a fair amount of prosperity well into the future," wrote
William D. Smith in the July 7, 1974, *New York Times.*

The impact of high oil prices in Europe and Japan has been far
more serious than in the United States. Western Europe faced a
balance-of-payments deficit of at least $20 billion in 1974, mostly
because of the higher price of oil. This does not tell the whole
story, however, because West Germany reaped a balance-of-
payments surplus of around $6 billion, so that the real impact on
France, Italy, and Britain, the hardest-hit countries, is greater. In
Japan the cost of foreign oil, which accounts for 80 percent of the
country's energy needs, *quadrupled.*

The British National Economic Development Office made a
grim assessment:

"Demand for automobiles will be reduced because the cost of
running a car will be 40 percent greater in 1977 than in 1973.

"Demand for clothing will decline because of permanently increased costs of fabrics produced from synthetic fibers, most of
which are made from petroleum products.

"Consumers will reduce their spending for major electrical
appliances, such as refrigerators and washing machines."

Food

No less profit-gouging than the policies of the oil monopolists—
and surely with an even more disastrous consequence for the
famine-stricken populations of the underdeveloped world—are the
policies of the U.S. food trusts. Huge shares of U.S. farm produce,
as has already been shown, are exported. These exports comprise
an even larger share of world food exports, so that the pricing
policies underlie world prices in food trade.

"Food is power," U.S. Secretary of Agriculture Earl Butz told
reporter William Robbins, stressing "the diplomatic leverage that
world dependence on American grain provides" (*New York
Times,* July 5, 1974).

The statistics of the International Monetary Fund (June 1974)
are equally eloquent:

The United States exports 45 percent of world corn exports (the
second largest exporter is Thailand with 5 percent). The wholesale price per bushel has risen from $1.37 in 1966 to $3.01 in
March 1974, a rise of 120 percent.

The United States exports 27 percent of world rice exports (with

Thailand again second at 11 percent). Rice sold for $8.30 per 100 pounds in New Orleans in 1967. The April 1974 price was $30, 261 percent higher.

The United States accounts for 94 percent of world soybean exports; prices have risen from $2.72 per bushel in 1967 to $6.34 in March 1974, up 133 percent.

U.S. wheat exports comprise 32 percent of world wheat exports (followed by Canada with 21 percent and Australia with 12 percent). Wheat in Kansas City rose from $1.79 a bushel in 1966 to $5.82 a bushel in February 1974, up 225 percent.

These fantastic price leaps have paralleled a huge increase in the volume of U.S. exports, beginning in 1972, so that the recent profit increases are even greater. The *Commodity Trade Statistics* published by the United Nations on wheat, for example, show that U.S. exports increased from 21.3 million metric tons in 1972 to an annual rate of 32 million tons in January-March 1973, a 50 percent rise in volume. In prices, the increase was from $1.4 billion for 1972 to an annual rate of $2.4 billion in the first three months of 1973, a 78 percent increase.

These trade statistics show that as famine-stricken underdeveloped countries were forced to purchase more wheat, the U.S. prices rose even further in proportion!

Thus, U.S. wheat exports to "developing countries" (a UN term) increased from 6.3 million metric tons in 1972 to an annual rate of 12.3 million metric tons in the first three months of 1973, a 94 percent increase. But the dollar price rose from $402 million to $1.1 billion, an increase of 181 percent!

A U.S. expert on "overseas development" told the *New York Times* (July 6, 1974, issue) that "for the 30 or 40 poorest countries—those with annual per capita incomes of not much more than $100—food import costs are too high. They have gone up too fast for them, primarily the grains which have to be imported by a large number of developing countries." The Washington official, Lester R. Brown of the Overseas Development Council, believed that 388 million people in the capitalist world were "fed insufficiently" in 1970, a figure which has most certainly increased with the droughts of the past two years.

The situation is likely to become exacerbated as fertilizer prices are driven up and grain production is even more severely limited in underdeveloped countries.

Worth noting, moreover, is a recent development in the U.S. beef trade. In the summer of 1974, prices began to fall back in agricultural livestock. Cattlemen sought U.S. *import controls* in order to keep beef prices up. Such controls have not so far been applied because beef imports have not yet been very great, although the Agriculture Department has been pressuring foreign countries to limit their beef exports to the U.S. and has been asking Canada to import more U.S. beef.

This example illustrates the "upward ratcheting" effect in world prices. So long as world demand for U.S. beef drove beef prices up in the United States, Washington sought free international trade conditions in order to keep the profits pouring in. When prices began to fall, however, protectionist moves were immediately initiated to prevent a return of prices to their old level.

Raw Materials

The hypocrisy bound up in the concept that raw-materials producer nations are somehow responsible for world inflation is limitless. All that one has to forget in this regard is the fact that the major imperialist powers control the marketing of raw materials—so that even when nationalizations are undertaken, profits are not seriously threatened. *But most of world raw materials continue to be owned by the major imperialist monopolies, above all by U.S. firms.* The inflation of the prices of other raw materials besides petroleum has provided a profit bonanza for the monopolists involved.

In the reports for the first quarter of 1974, *Business Week* magazine listed metals as the most profitable U.S. sector, with an industry-wide average increase of 94 percent from the first quarter of 1973. Fuel stood second with an 82 percent increase. Among the corporations reporting were Phelps Dodge (copper and brass), up 41 percent; Kennecott Copper, up 42 percent; American Metal Climax (coal, potash, iron, copper, zinc, lead, molybdenum), up 59 percent; Anaconda (copper), up 98 percent; Kaiser Aluminum and Chemical, up 147 percent; American Smelting and Refining (copper, gold, silver, lead) up 101 percent; Reynolds Metals (aluminum), up 454 percent.

Interestingly, the rise in copper prices has been so great that Anaconda reports its 1973 sales of $1.3 billion almost equaled the 1969 sales of $1.4 billion, before its lucrative Chuquicamata and El Salvador "properties" were nationalized in Chile.

This multinational copper trust held in 1973:

Anaconda Canada Ltd.; 75 percent ownership of the open-pit Caribou mine in New Brunswick; and Anaconda Electronics Ltd., Vancouver, British Columbia.

Also "a larger investment in Mexico," according to its 1973 annual report, "than in any other nation outside the United States," with 49 percent ownership or less of: Compañía Minera de Cananea, Cobre de Mexico, Condumex, Nacional de Cobre, and Swecomex; Anaconda Australia, Inc.; Anaconda B.V., Amsterdam, the Netherlands; Fios e Cabos Plásticos do Brasil and S.A. Marvin (brass and copper products), both in Rio de Janeiro.

Anaconda's multinational holdings are typical. A similar pattern exists for the other corporations except that in some cases (molybdenum and bauxite, for example) the sources are almost entirely outside of the United States.

The drain of profits continues from the underdeveloped world. It is not these countries that profit from the inflation of raw materials prices—yet they do have to pay for inflated food prices.

II

As prices rose the world over, U.S. capitalism reaped unprecedented benefits. Holdings in five of the seven major international petroleum corporations, a commanding position in vitally needed world food exports, global monopolization of raw materials—all contributed to record-breaking profits for American corporations in 1973–74. This was a central objective of the escalated offensive in world trade and finance signaled by Nixon's "New Economic Policy" in 1971.

Furthermore, it is clear that one of the important causes of inflation lies precisely in the double devaluation of the dollar decided on by the Nixon administration. By May 1973 the Federal Reserve Board could calculate the following appreciations of foreign currencies against the dollar as compared to April 1971:

Australia	up 26.3%
Belgium-Luxembourg	up 27.7%
Britain	up 6.4%
Canada	up 0.8%
France	up 25.0%
Germany	up 31.6%
Italy	up 6.2%
Japan	up 36.2%

Although in the spring of 1973 the dollar was being buffeted by a new wave of selling in international markets, Federal Reserve

Board member Daane testified that "the outlook for the U.S. international payments position, and hence for the dollar, is considerably better now than it has been for some time.

"The outlook has been greatly improved by the exchange rate realignments of 1970–71 and early 1973. Altogether, the U.S. dollar has been effectively devalued against all other currencies by about 17 percent since mid-1970, and by substantially more than that against our strongest competitors. This is a very large adjustment, which greatly improves the international competitiveness of U.S. goods."

The devaluations in December 1971 and February 1973 succeeded in cheapening the prices of U.S. goods relative to those of Washington's major overseas rivals. U.S. exports once again were able to rise above imports. Concentration on the export trade greatly increased. *Business Week* magazine reported July 6, 1974, that "U.S. exports of goods and services, as a percentage of GNP, have almost doubled—to nearly 8% in the last 10 years. For merchandise alone—excluding services, which are less mobile—exports now account for 12% of U.S. goods production."

The increasing export trade mounted on two devaluations of the dollar is a key cause of the rapid U.S. inflation that erupted in 1973.

Dollar devaluation both directly and indirectly contributed to higher prices in the United States. Its direct contribution comes from raising the prices of foreign goods in the U.S. market—after all, one of the main reasons for the devaluation to begin with.

The appreciation of foreign currencies against the dollar automatically raises the price of foreign goods in the U.S. market. A Japanese businessman complained to *Business Week*: "The rising cost of wages and materials . . . coupled with the revaluation of the yen, have already cost Toyota and Nissan their price advantage in the U.S. auto market, and by 1975 the electronics industry will be in the same fix" (July 6, 1974).

But this is actually doubly inflationary. It not only means that cheaper cars are no longer available to U.S. consumers from abroad. *It also allows American corporations to raise their prices on cars.*

When the edge is taken off foreign competition, and especially (as shown by the complaint of the Japanese executive) when capitalist rivals are hit even harder by inflation than companies in the United States, the "barriers" to price rises topple. Since "price controls" were officially lifted in April 1974, U.S. auto prices have been zooming upward.

A second important industry in which this effect is visible is steel. Foreign competition had in some cases formerly caused U.S. firms to actually cut steel prices; today they are jacking up prices to unprecedented levels. Between April and July 1974 the U.S. Steel Corporation raised its prices *23 percent.*

Auto industry figures in June 1974 recorded the impact on foreign competition as a recession in the U.S. economy began to undermine car sales:

"Sales by the four United States auto makers were estimated at 765,147 last month, a decline of 21.2 percent from 971,304 in May of last year.

"Sales of imports were off an even sharper 32.7 percent, to 115,000 from 171,000 in May, 1973. The market share of the imports was down to 13.1 percent, a new low for the year, which started off with imports capturing 18.6 percent of January sales" (*New York Times,* June 5, 1974).

Thus devaluations—far from "only influencing foreign trade," as the commentators pretend—have an important inflationary effect on domestic prices (and this is precisely because domestic prices are inextricably linked to world prices through foreign trade).

Shortages

A second important factor in the present inflation—the appearance of shortages in the U.S. economy—is also inseparable from the effects of devaluation. It has been asked: How can there be shortages in the United States, particularly when a central feature of world capitalism is generalized *overproduction,* with its consequent global struggle to find markets for goods and investment?

Yet this contradictory phenomenon is a consequence of the very character of monopoly rule. Monopolists deliberately curtail production to keep prices up. The United States witnessed the remarkable phenomenon of the oil firms virtually halting refinery building over a period of years, with all the consequent price rises and profit-gouging effects of the "energy crisis."

Under the impact of intensified world competition, it is likely that such occurrences will become more general. A country that has higher inflation rates and higher profits will suck goods and investments out of other countries.

On a national scale inflation redistributes wealth towards the upper strata, tending to limit the consumption of more expensive consumer goods to those who can afford to pay for them—especially including the very layers that most profit from these sales at inflated prices. On an international scale inflation redistributes the wealth of the semicolonial and lesser imperialist nations towards the more powerful centers of world capitalism.

This can result in shortages—and consequently in driving the prices up where the shortages occur. Inflation breeds further inflation and it all the more reinforces national and international inequalities.

The question of tempo is also vitally important. The generalized saturation of markets that came as the postwar expansion of European and Japanese capitalism reached its peak does not preclude the continuation of business cycles within this overall context. The years 1970 and 1971 saw recessions in most advanced capitalist countries, but the selling off of inventories, dampening of wage increases, and government deficit spending paved the way for a new world upswing.

In fact 1972–73 saw a simultaneous rise of the economies of all the major powers, and this in itself sharpened inflationary tendencies. That is because prices always tend to rise more rapidly on the upswing side of a business cycle. As production is expanding and more and more workers are hired, demand tends to run ahead of supply, pulling up prices. When this occurred on a global scale in the last two years, the result was a massive upsurge of demand, spurring world trade. In the words of *Business Week* (July 6, 1974), "Buyers all over the world have been scrambling for supplies of everything from sugar to machine tools, irrespective of national boundaries."

But this happened when two dollar devaluations had greatly cheapened U.S. goods. The result, as U.S. exports soared, was sudden major shortages in the American economy and drastic price increases!

In the May 1974 issue of *Fortune* magazine, Lewis Beman vividly described the long "pre-NEP" ("New Economic Policy") period of stagnating investment under the blows of world competition. In that "era of lagging profits,"

> sinking stock prices, and record-breaking interest rates, the capital-budgeting exercise had taken on a new character. Beleaguered by complaining shareholders and anxious investment bankers, managers have been torn between the natural urge to conquer new markets and the even more primitive instinct for self-preservation.
>
> Living in this new environment, businessmen have understandably behaved more like managers and less like entrepreneurs. They have

gravitated toward what might be called *managerial* investments—in which financial results can be calibrated down to the nearest basis point and justified to the most conservative of bankers. They have shied away from *entrepreneurial* investments—in which the commitment is substantial, the costs uncertain, the payout lengthy, and the risk of loss agonizingly real.

Under world conditions of saturated markets, investment is retarded because a big new investment *might not* find markets for its products. But the devaluation of the dollar, combined with a rising world demand that was fueled by deficits—especially in the United States itself—radically altered the situation. Beman writes:

> The over-valued dollar had repressed the growth of many producers: directly, by creating new competition for them in the U.S. market, and indirectly, by eroding the overseas markets of their manufacturing customers. It took the double devaluation of the dollar—which raised the price of foreign goods by as much as 50 percent—to reverse these devastating trends. But when the reversal finally took place, basic manufacturers in the U.S. suddenly found that they had the lowest prices in the world. And they also had the longest list of customers.

In March 1974 the list of industries with long backlogs of orders included steel, zinc, forgings, castings, motors, electronic components, fuels, lumber, bearings, engines, valves, paper, resins, benzene, caustic soda, soda ash, waxes. It was "by far the worst shortage situation since the 1920s," one steel executive told Beman. It was also the opportunity for unprecedented price and profit rises.

This phenomenon was most apparent to Americans, of course, in the food industry, where the sudden upsurge of exports helped to create shortages driving agricultural prices to record highs beginning in the spring of 1973. It has been estimated that from November 1972 to August 1973, 64 percent of the increase in U.S. wholesale prices resulted directly or indirectly from the increase in agricultural prices.

"Keynesianism" Stymied

The foregoing effects of devaluation and sharpened trade warfare do not in and of themselves completely explain inflation. For inflation to take place there must be not only an increased demand and monopoly conditions whereby price increases can be imposed on markets, there must also be an increase of the money supply to fuel the new higher-priced purchases. But the world money supply is growing on an unprecedented scale—and it is this phenomenon that is sowing doubts about the ability of governments to bring the inflationary crisis under control.

The whole essence of "Keynesian" policies is to *inflate* economies in order to keep up purchasing power. This was thought to be the lesson of the depression of the 1930s. "The unseen hand could fumble, and if nothing was done about it, the Marxian prophecy of total collapse might come to pass," *Business Week* said June 29, 1974. "The remedy Keynes suggested—aggressive government spending—became the almost universal prescription for economic policymakers."

Moreover Keynes was completely conscious of the inflationary effects of deficit spending. He argued that insofar as inflation was detrimental to workers' incomes, it had the advantage from the capitalists' standpoint that while workers fight back against direct cuts of their nominal wages, they tend not to resist the hidden slashes of their real wages through monetary inflation. Said Keynes, "It would be impracticable to resist every reduction of real wages, due to a change in the purchasing-power of money which affects all workers alike; and in fact reductions of real wages arising in this way are not, as a rule, resisted unless they proceed to an extreme degree" (*The General Theory of Employment, Interest, and Money,* p. 14).

But in the Keynesian model, the national government makes up its deficits in downturns by running surplus budgets during the upswing. Moreover, it is a parochial view, a model for one country. Keynes did not foresee what would happen if, as in the United States, deficits occurred with increasing frequency even in times of "peace," nor did he see the eventuality of simultaneous deficit spending across the capitalist globe.

Leonard Silk wrote in the June 26, 1974, *New York Times:* "Among the casualties of the present inflation, economic stagnation, soaring interest rates and slumping stock and bond markets are major elements of modern economic theory." Silk pointed out the weakness of the three main schools: *Fiscal doctrine* advocates cutting taxes or increasing expenditures in order to create full employment; *monetary theory* advocates that the Federal Reserve expand the money supply in order to assure steady growth; the "third major economic doctrine . . . was the idea that *floating exchange rates,* free to move up or down in relation to changing national balance-of-payments surpluses or deficits, would restore equilibrium to the world monetary system.

"Floating exchange rates would also liberate national economic policy from external pressures—for instance pressure to deflate the economy and accept higher unemployment to support too high a fixed currency rate . . ." (emphasis added).

The result of this policy in relation to the United States has already been examined. Floating the U.S. dollar, in effect allowing it to be devalued twice, stabilized the dollar at the cost of rampant inflation. ". . . All three of these doctrines," Silk observed, "far from being symmetrical as advertised, have proved to be highly assymetrical—that is, biased toward inflation."

Moreover, it is not only the United States that prefers "moderate inflation" to the politically even more unpopular regimen of high unemployment. In 1971-73 every capitalist power incurred inflation-producing budget deficits for all three of the years except France, which ran a budget surplus in 1972.

Simultaneous economic expansion was accompanied by an even more rapid expansion of the money supply, resulting in a global expansion of the inflation rate. Keynesianism "works" on a national scale if the surplus purchasing power pumped into one country can, to some extent, be absorbed elsewhere in the world system. This was an important aspect of the U.S. economy within the context of the postwar world. Continuous U.S. deficits, above all to support the military machine, were not acutely inflationary as long as world capitalism was generally expanding.

Today, nations are following parallel inflationary policies, and inflation is rapidly "exported" from one country to another. Wherever the inflation rate is highest, high prices draw goods toward that country, pulling up prices elsewhere. Moreover, the resulting increase in world trade tends to draw the movement of world economies into closer synchronization.

This is especially reinforced by the large size of the U.S. economy relative to the world economy, so that the movement of the U.S. economy tends to pull that of the others toward it. If 1972-73 saw a parallel rise of the economies of the major powers, in 1974 the world was already heading into its second international recession in the postwar period, barely two years after the first, with the danger of its being far graver.

The phenomenon of world inflation—whether it results from domestic budgetary policies aimed at artificially expanding purchasing power, or from manipulations in international exchange rates, again aimed at an artificial expansion of markets— expresses the inability of the capitalist system to thrive without continuous expansion of productive investment. Credit is expanded, and paper money is pumped into the world system to make up for the slack. This is a risky business.

Liquidity Crisis

"Credit inflation" is especially dangerous when, as is the case today, the world economy is beginning to turn toward recession. In mid-1974 (June 30) the *New York Times* reported that "there has been a slowing of the growth rate in Western Europe, with some countries (Britain in particular) teetering on the brink of recession. . . .

"Real output, after making allowance for price increases, actually declined in the United States by 6 per cent in the first quarter, while the inflation rate is running over 10 per cent."

A "liquidity crisis" inevitably occurs as a capitalist economy turns toward downswing. The threat is that this could occur internationally.

As corporations begin to find their sales declining, they are forced to borrow to finance swollen inventories of overproduced goods. Moreover, especially in the United States at present, the beginning of an economic downturn has been accompanied by an *upsurge of capital spending.*

This historically unusual event undoubtedly corresponds to the newfound conviction of U.S. capital that it can, with sufficient cudgel in world affairs, continue to maintain its superiority in world markets. If two devaluations of the dollar brought the profit bonanza they did—why not more protectionism if and when necessary? A McGraw-Hill survey of business investment plans for 1974-77, released May 3, 1974, found a "notable 19% increase [in 1974] over 1973 spending. . . . Capacity is expected to grow 16% between the end of 1974 and 1977." It is more than likely that these figures will be sharply revised in a downward direction before 1977.

Nevertheless, the concurrence of heavy corporate demand for funds to finance inventories and for investment funds, riding on top of a 10 percent annual inflation rate, is driving interest rates to their highest levels in American history. Abroad, with even greater inflation rates, the interest rates are all the higher. In mid-1974, overseas inflation rates included 19 percent in France, 20 percent in Singapore, 26 percent in Japan, and 35 percent in Brazil.

The widely varying inflation rates have already led the prestigious "Committee of Twenty," representing the leading central bankers of the capitalist world, to abandon attempts to build a successor to Bretton Woods, after two years of meetings. Any form of fixed currency exchange rates is inconceivable under the tension created by divergent inflationary trends. Floating rates, continuously modifying in the give and take of exacerbated world competition, are the order of the day.

"The Loans Are Eternal"

In this explosive situation, an international credit collapse becomes increasingly possible. All of the world's major banks are ever more deeply interlinked in the global expansion of credit. The bankruptcy of one enterprise quickly influences the rest, since they are all up to their chins in the same game—each has lent funds to others.

The collapses in June and July 1974 of the Franklin National Bank in the U.S. and of I.D. Herstatt in West Germany were symbolic. "Herstatt," *Business Week* reported July 6, 1974, "lost an estimated $200-million in foreign exchange dealings and was forced to close. . . . The Herstatt failure is proving costly for other banks that dealt with it, and it threw the financial markets of Europe into a panic. The rate on one-month Eurodollars jumped from 12.9% to 14.3% in a single day, and the foreign exchange markets on the Continent were nearly paralyzed."

Equally significant, however, were the paths followed to salvage these wrecks. In the United States, the Federal Reserve Board issued more than $1 billion in credits to Franklin. A consortium of world banks promised to back up the Herstatt failure. Thus the only answer to such problems is to expand the credit bubble even more.

On a state scale this takes on all the more importance. As government deficits expand, as state powers increasingly tap capital markets for funds, the problem can reach truly intolerable proportions. *Business Week* declared: "Eurobankers are already edgy about the billions they have lent to governments that may be pushed to bankruptcy by oil bills. . . .

"Italy is a real problem. The Italians, who face a $12-billion trade deficit this year, have already borrowed heavily in Eurocurrency markets. Now, says Vice-President David Devlin of First National City Bank: 'Italy can't borrow any more even with a government guarantee.'"

So far as the "Arab oil billions" are concerned, the real problem is rarely mentioned. After all, of what possible harm can it be to have up to $100 billion in investment funds available to pour into the world economy? *The problem is precisely the absence of long-term investment potentials. It is the clearest indication in international finance of the end of the long-term expansion.*

Business Week expressed it in these terms: "The main channel for recycled wealth is the vast Eurodollar market, which has probably handled at least $15-billion in oil money since the price went up. But the money is going to only a relative handful of institutions, chiefly the London branches of giant U.S. banks, and it is coming in only for very short periods. And short-term deposits are a pain because borrowers want the money for long periods. Says one banker ruefully: 'The money is in overnight, the loans are eternal.'"

They are words that could easily presage a banking collapse on the order of the 1930s. On one side corporations (and governments!), beset by financial difficulties, want loans. But the banks, precisely because of these difficulties, demand high interest. At some point these needs can diverge too widely.

Deflation

With parallel "Keynesian" policies of leading capitalist governments overinflating national economies, there are indications of a further parallel turn of these governments toward the "classical" solution of *deflation*. Government spending must be cut. Taxes must be raised. Workers must be laid off in sufficient numbers to dampen their wage demands, ultimately decreasing the level of wage increases, and opening to the respective powers needed room for maneuver in world competition.

This is perhaps the main source of embarrassment to bourgeois economics. *Business Week* cites the case of Professor Tobin of Yale, a veteran presidential economic adviser and author of *The New Economics One Decade Older,* who puts the blame on politicians. No leaders of either the Democrats or Republicans, claims Tobin, has ever dared to admit to the people that price stability and full employment are incompatible goals under capitalism. But it is hardly an exaggeration to say that this insuperable contradiction of capitalism is not featured prominently in economics textbooks either.

Whatever their private and public second thoughts, the leaders of world capitalism are simultaneously moving toward international deflation, just as their economies simultaneously surged upward two years ago. This was the price world bankers demanded to come to Italy's rescue. In the United States the Federal Reserve is following stringent tight-money policies that can only end in a further sharp curtailment of production.

But this is the danger. When workers are being laid off on an international scale, when purchasing power is falling across the globe, the result could be a worldwide depression.

In a recent widely noted article, the London *Economist* reported from a Paris meeting of the Organization for Economic Cooperation and Development that the countries "prescribed a large dose of exactly the wrong deflationary medicine for a world that is sliding alarmingly quickly towards a slump."

The *Economist* continued: "Forty-five years after 1929, with the forward prospect for world demand rather more deflationary than it seemed to be in 1929-30, it is almost inconceivable that the majority of the 24 leading countries of the world should be intent on following a more anti-Keynesian policy than it did then. But this is what is happening."

The *Economist* wants even further inflation. It is an easy recommendation for the City of London to make with the Labour Party in power. Yet it is precisely the sharp intensification of inflation in Britain, the deep cuts into the standard of living of workers, and their upsurge of militancy on the picket lines that brought the new Labour government into power to begin with. Only with the utmost cynicism can The *Economist* suggest policies to other governments that would be catastrophic to their own.

Go It Alone Over the Brink

But the dilemma is inescapable. As the crisis of world imperialism deepens, there are no alternatives for each government but inflationary or recessionary policies or both, with governments skirting closer to disaster on both sides. Inflation spreads like fire from one country to the next; deflation threatens to bring about a worldwide economic slowdown. Both of them lead to sharpening class battles that cut away still further the competitive abilities of rival powers.

And here is the crux of the matter:

No matter how far-flung their multinational investments, and no matter how much world capitalism increasingly comes to depend on expanded world trade, in the last analysis capitalisms are national. The basis of power of the competing ruling classes lies in their own states and in the control over "their own" workers that the repressive governmental apparatus makes possible.

The editors of the *New York Times* said on July 2, 1974, "The real question is whether there is or can be a common Western purpose at all. Or whether, in dealing with the explosive energy and petro-dollar crisis, go-it-alone policies will be followed that could destroy the benefits of three decades of politico-economic cooperation, endanger the common defense structure and set off a worldwide depression."

But what else is international competition except "go-it-alone"? Every ingredient of the world crisis expresses *national needs.* Currencies are devalued in order to carve out bigger world markets. (The European Common Market can no longer even maintain a common EEC float.) Governments run deficits to shore up their own economies. The meaning of outright protectionism, as most recently shown in the case of Italy, is obvious.

On a small scale, as in the example of backing the loans of I.D. Herstatt, or even bailing out Italy on a short-run basis, international capitalism can unite to protect specific interests. But it is utopian to believe that this can take place on a much wider scale.

Lenin stressed that the fundamental problem for imperialism is the contradiction between the expansive needs of capital on an international scale and national boundaries. This is the essence of the present inflationary-recessionary world crisis.

A further series of protectionist measures in world trade and parallel deflationary policies on a world scale, if carried too far, would lead just where they led in the 1930s—to drastic production cutbacks and massive unemployment.

The imperialist governments will not plunge blindly into this catastrophe. They turned to the ideas of Keynes because they believed, with good reason, that capitalism could not survive another international depression. Nevertheless, the end of the long-term boom and the intensification of world competition have released forces that can no longer be contained within the safe limits envisioned by Lord Keynes. Rising unemployment and explosive inflation have become the inescapable "solutions."

Do Mideast Oil Billions
Threaten the World?

"A grim, new mood is developing in Washington that military intervention may be necessary to bring down the price of oil and save the West from economic ruin," syndicated columnist Jack Anderson wrote from Washington on November 8, 1974.

"Oil is the lifeblood of the industrial West. A growing number of policymakers now agree that the United States cannot stand by while a few recklessly greedy potentates interfere with the normal flow of our lifeblood. . . . Our sources say the President is willing to use U.S. military power as a last resort to prevent the oil cartel from causing disastrous economic and political dislocations in the West."

The "leak" to Anderson was followed in the first week of January by a trial balloon lofted by no one less than Secretary of State Henry Kissinger. In an interview in the January 13, 1975, issue of *Business Week* magazine he announced for the first time, "I am not saying that there's not circumstances where we would not use force."

These trial balloons have been floated several times in the press and on TV in recent months. The mighty United States is said to be at the mercy of irresponsible Arab sheiks. The inflation, indeed the whole economic crisis that threatens to extend into an international depression, is the fault of the "oil cartel."

War threats against the Arab countries and Iran emanate from such generally staid circles as the U.S. Council on Foreign Relations. In the CFR's quarterly journal, *Foreign Affairs,* Walter J. Levy, a well-known spokesman for the U.S. oil trusts, wrote in July 1974 that "unrestrained exercise of their oil and money power by the producing countries presupposes that the importing countries will continue to acquiesce and remain passive, even if the world's economic and political stability is at stake. This cannot be a safe basis upon which the producing countries could proceed. If the worst is to be avoided, the producing countries must be made to recognize the danger of pursuing such a course."

The imperialist propaganda campaign has distinctly racist overtones. On the one hand, spokesmen for the most powerful and ruthless empire in all history, responsible for the murder of untold thousands in Indochina, wax indignant when a few desperately impoverished countries, long plundered of their natural resources, begin to collect a substantial share of the revenues produced from their soil. On the other hand there is a conscious effort to identify the Arab oil-producing states with the dispossessed Palestinian people, who have neither land nor oil but who have been the target of reactionary anti-Arab tirades by the Zionist rulers of Israel and their supporters in the U.S.

A Zionist demonstration in front of the United Nations on November 4, 1974, which attracted 60,000 to 100,000 persons, heard Democratic Party liberal Ramsey Clark call for a multinational effort "to liberate the world from the tyranny of Arab oil." New York Republican Senator Jacob Javits declared that the UN vote to hear the Palestine Liberation Organization was "an historic act of diplomatic infamy." AFL-CIO secretary Lane Kirkland urged Washington to confront the Arab oil-producing countries, and if necessary America's European allies as well. "If we are to stand alone with Israel," the assistant to George Meany said, "we might as well know it now."

The same day, *Time* magazine appeared with a front-cover story on the shah of Iran entitled "The Emperor of Oil."

And most ominously, as Yasir Arafat presented the viewpoint of the PLO in New York and his Arab supporters were clubbed and hosed by Israeli cops in Jerusalem, Israeli pronouncements and military moves in the Middle East began to follow an all-too-familiar pattern: Tel Aviv's preparation for preemptive war.

The fact is that the world is threatened by another war in the Middle East. The respective sides are armed as never before. The mass communications media in the West are beating the drums against the Palestinians and denouncing the "Arab oil money" that allegedly stands behind them. The holders of Arab and Iranian petrodollars are accused of everything from subverting peace in the Middle East to seeking the destruction of the capitalist world economy.

It is crucially important to understand the falsity of this propaganda. There is the real danger of an economic crisis in the capitalist world on a scale unseen since the 1930s. There is the danger of a new war in the Middle East—Brezhnev and Ford through their policy of détente are trying to prevent it from breaking out, and bartering away the rights of the Palestinians in the process. But as the October war in 1973 showed, agreements between Washington and Moscow to preserve the status quo do not abolish the laws of the class struggle. And a new confrontation in the Middle East always has the potential of escalating into nuclear conflagration. The central blame for the pressing dangers, however, lies in the policies of world imperialism, and above all in the policies of Washington, not in the activities of the oil-producing nations.

The "Oil Weapon" and the Accumulation of "Petrodollars"

To expose the propaganda of the imperialists, it is necessary to begin by underlining the far-reaching turn in international affairs signaled by the "energy crisis," the October war of 1973, the oil boycott and raising of oil prices, and the disarray of the imperialist powers that these events precipitated. The London-based International Institute for Strategic Studies, a "think tank" for imperialist policies, opened its 1973 *Strategic Survey* with the opinion that "the successful use of the oil weapon by the Arab states in connection with the Middle East war of October produced the greatest shock, the most potent sense of a new era, of any event of recent years."

Three of the new factors mentioned by the survey are worth citing:

This was the first time that major industrial states had to bow to pressure from pre-industrial ones.

Second, the special vulnerability of the industrial transforming regions, dependent on imported energy, was vividly shown up. When bipolarity [the predominance in world politics of the U.S. and the USSR] broke down with China's return to the diplomatic fold in 1971, it became fashionable to argue that world power had become "pentagonal." True, the super-powers were in a military class by themselves (to which China alone might one day accede), but the massive economic powers like **Japan** and the European Community might, in the increasingly civilian world, exercise influence which placed them in an almost equivalent category. However, the energy crisis demonstrated the *weakness of the European Community, Japan and, to a lesser extent, Eastern Europe,* and hence the limitations of this view. . . .

Third, the energy crisis, which was politically an Arab-Western one, *found the Western powers spectacularly divided and quite unprepared to face the strains.* [emphasis added]

As important as these three factors are, in every case the experts have concealed the most important *cause,* namely, the drive of U.S. imperialism to maintain its postwar position of hegemony in the world capitalist market.

For the oil-producing countries were able to pressure Europe and Japan into accepting higher oil prices *only because this pressure dovetailed with the aims of the American ruling class.* It is true that the energy crisis demonstrated the weakness of Europe and Japan, but it is most importantly a weakness vis-à-vis the United States. The exploitation of this weakness is a central aim of Washington's foreign policy.

Perhaps this is best illustrated by the argument over "petrodollars" itself. Most crudely stated, the pile-up of enormous reserves in the Organization of Petroleum Exporting Countries (OPEC) nations as a result of oil revenues is supposed to constitute a monetary crisis of untold proportions: "The problem," says a *New York Times* editorial November 11, 1974, "is that the oil-producing countries cannot spend more than a fraction of their earnings. They are piling up unspendable claims on the rest of the world so fast that by the end of next year they are expected to total more than $120 billion, twice the net U.S. foreign assets at the end of last year."

Newsweek magazine put it this way November 18, 1974: "U.S. officials estimate that Saudi Arabia's reserves will rise to as much as $35 billion in 1975. By this measurement, at least, that could make the desert nation the world's leading financial power."

It is surely worth noting that while total OPEC reserves obviously refer to other countries in addition to the Middle East (notably Venezuela and Nigeria), the propaganda is aimed almost entirely at the Arab countries and Iran. For their own reasons the imperialists do not direct their fire at Black Africa or Latin America at this time. Also worth noting is the even less mentioned fact that both *Britain* and *Norway* envision levying royalties on North Sea oil every bit on a par with present OPEC taxation.

But the mere accumulation of monetary reserves outside of the imperialist centers does not automatically produce world monetary problems. They can create a shortage of world capital if they are simply hoarded; or they can lead to runs on the dollar if large amounts are suddenly transferred out of dollar holdings. If they are spent on goods and services in the imperialist countries, however, they can have a stimulating effect on the capitalist economy, and deposits in Western banks provide a source of further lendings by the banks. Concretely, how are the reserves of the oil-producing states being held and used?

They are central bank holdings of international means of payment—gold, major world currencies, and Special Drawing Rights (SDRs) of the International Monetary Fund. So far as the Middle East reserves are concerned, *they are above all holdings of the currencies of the major Western powers.* These currencies are not physically held by the central banks of the Middle East for the most part, but exist as deposits in Western banks and treasury notes of Western governments.

Figures that have been released differ, but the pattern is comparable. According to the *New York Times,* November 21, 1974, "Twenty per cent of the funds earned in the first 10 months [of 1974] was invested in United States banks or marketable United States Government securities. 40 per cent was in the Eurodollar market, 15 per cent in the pound sterling, 8 per cent went into other Western European and Japanese currencies, and the balance was divided among international institutions and other investments."

Whatever the precise figures, most petrodollars are deposited in U.S. banks, or are invested in U.S. Treasury securities, or in the Eurodollar market. (Eurodollars are dollars on deposit and available for loan in Europe, primarily through the London-based subsidiaries of U.S. banks.) These are conservative investments, to be sure, and that is one of the things that irritate Western bankers. But to say that they constitute a crisis in and of themselves is a complete distortion of reality.

In the first place, they are primarily in dollars because dollars are the main currency of world capitalist finance. If the dollar is shaky, and the Middle East nations unload some of their dollar holdings, they will only be following a precedent long established by U.S. multinational corporations abroad. It is not the unloading of dollars to begin with but the uncontrolled inflation in the United States, constantly threatening to weaken the dollar, that throws international finance into crisis.

Theoretically, in fact, these dollar holdings should be helpful to the international monetary system by providing funds to countries with balance-of-payments deficits. Gerald A. Pollack, a senior economic adviser for Exxon, ironically argues in *Foreign Affairs,* April 1974: "Britain and Italy, through borrowing by their public authorities, have already drawn on this large pool of international liquidity. . . . And on January 31 France announced intentions to borrow around $1.5 billion in the Eurocurrency market specifically for the purpose of helping to pay for the higher cost of oil imports." But the problem is that international liquidity is provided at interest. Not only Middle East central banks but those in the United States insist on repayment. The nub of the question is: Can Britain and Italy repay their borrowings—*plus interest?*

To the extent that petrodollars are invested in long-term stocks abroad—and so far this is quite minor—they cannot also be said to constitute a monetary crisis. Isn't it actually a good thing for the capitalists of West Germany that Iran is willing to invest upwards of $100 million in Krupp?

And it is precisely on this point that the imperialist chauvinism of the "petrodollar crisis" argument shows through. The imperialists, who have taken over companies in every corner of the world through their foreign investments, do not want their own firms taken over by foreign capital. Insofar as one can speak of a crisis, it is a political and not an economic one: how to prevent the Arab and Iranian interlopers from using the normal and legal mechanism of the stock market to acquire commanding shares in major U.S. and European corporations—such as the $8 billion Arab investment in IBM reportedly under consideration.

With unlimited hypocrisy, however, the imperialists turn around and attack petrodollar investments for being short-term rather than long. But this is putting the cart before the horse. The Middle Eastern central bankers do not invest long-term because, in the deepening world crisis of capitalism, there are not good long-term prospects. With characteristic understatement, the *Middle East Economic Digest* (MEED) declared August 9, 1974, "Suitable investment opportunities have not yet been found."

The "unspendable claims on the rest of the world" that the *New York Times* complains about are unspendable because, among other reasons, the New York stock and bond markets offer little attraction. So the pile-up of OPEC moneys in reserves rather than productive investment is not a cause of the crisis of capitalism, it is a direct result of it.

What the imperialists would really like, nevertheless, is not long-term productive investments (in which they would be surrendering ownership to foreign investors) but long-term loans to nations such as Italy that the imperialists themselves would rather not lend money to! David Rockefeller, chairman of the Chase Manhattan Bank, told the *Middle East Economic Digest* August 16, 1974, that North American banks had provided balance-of-payments loans worth about $20 billion since the start of the year. He said countries will "reach a point where credit is no longer available on acceptable terms and they will have to cut back their oil imports."

In other words, not only are the OPEC bankers ungrateful enough to decline to lend their money to bad credit risks and take them off Rockefeller's hands, but by putting their money in Rockefeller's bank and themselves expecting interest for it they compel him to make the less desirable loans, if anyone is going to. Petrodollars are being "recycled" rather than hoarded, just as the imperialist bankers have demanded, but in a way that forces New York and London to take the risks. Like Pentagonese, the new-speak terminology of the banking world usually hides more than it explains. In this case the sudden passion for "recycling" has already dissipated. Alfred Hayes, president of the Federal Reserve Bank of New York, told the *New York Times* November 20, 1974, that he "regards the term 'recycling' as a misnomer—or worse—for the problem at hand, because it conceals 'the basic question of who should assume the credit risk in lending to the countries beset with economic difficulties'"!

Lost in this exchange is the fact that petrodollars are in New York and London because that is where the strongest banks are, which can offer the highest interest rates at least risk. If Rockefeller doesn't want to get the OPEC deposits, let him lower interest rates and allow the funds to go to his competitors. If he doesn't want to lend money to Italy, then, in his capacity as a head of Exxon as well as of the Chase Manhattan Bank, he should lower the price of world oil.

The possibility exists that simultaneous recessions in the advanced capitalist countries will deepen into a world depression that would cause a liquidity crisis in the extreme—that is, the urgent demand of corporations and governments for cash and the refusal of bankers to take the risk.

Under these circumstances the imperialists might very well decide to freeze petrodollar reserves under the pretext that they are *causing* the liquidity crisis. In fact, however, both petrodollar reserves and the liquidity crisis are *effects* of the threatened world slowdown of capitalist industrial production.

Petrodollars are flowing into U.S. and strong European currencies because these nations are faring better in interimperialist competition. They are not going into loans for Italy and the even harder hit semicolonial capitalist nations because these nations are faring worse in interimperialist competition. Thus petrodollar flows are not the cause of interimperialist contradictions; they are governed by them and are entirely subordinate to them.

The Underlying Cause of High Oil Prices

Even more important, higher oil prices did not fundamentally originate in decisions made by OPEC nations, but in the changing conditions of international competition. The "energy crisis" erupted *before* the October war. It reflects the *long-term drive of the United States to raise world oil prices,* and no matter how much they carp about high prices, the oil trusts have no intention of ever lowering oil prices to their pre-1973 levels.

What will fundamentally determine oil prices now and in the future is the level at which alternative energy forms as well as alternative sources of oil can be profitably produced. Oil prices will rise toward but will not exceed this level. And it is the drive of the U.S. oil giants to strengthen their hold on alternative sources—and in doing this, for one thing, to lessen their dependence on Middle East oil—that made higher oil prices a central objective of U.S. policy over a long period before the October war.

Moreover, the imperialists have long foreseen that an inevitable result of the rise of the colonial revolution in the postwar period would be a curtailment of their ability to control world prices of raw materials. It is one of the reasons they take the independence movement in Southeast Asia so seriously, an area where future oil production has high priority.

In a typical article urging higher oil prices three months before the October war, mining executive Carroll L. Wilson wrote in *Foreign Affairs* in July 1973: "The objectives of my proposal are to achieve, by 1985: first, the independence of the United States from critical reliance on imports of energy in any form . . . second, energy costs below some target level. . . . I suggest as a goal keeping energy costs for premium fuels such as gas or oil below $1.00 per million BTU. This is equivalent to oil at $6.00 a barrel, roughly twice present prices, or to gas at $1.00 per thousand cubic feet, twice present wellhead prices on new contracts."

A more frequently given figure was $10 as the upper limit for oil. In August 1973 Nadim Pachachi, former secretary-general of

OPEC, predicted that Arabian–Persian Gulf oil would go up to $10 a barrel by 1980. It reached this point several months later in the aftermath of the October war.

Long before this, the U.S. oil trusts had diversified into alternative energy sources. Two of the three largest U.S. coal companies (and five of the ten largest) are subsidiaries of the American oil giants. They control 45 percent of known uranium reserves and own four out of five plants for reprocessing used nuclear fuel elements. In 1970, of the twenty-five largest U.S. oil companies, eighteen had positions in oil shale, eleven in coal, eighteen in uranium, and seven in tar sands.

In *Asia, Oil Politics and the Energy Crisis* (1974), Leon Howell and Michael Morrow write:

> The technology—primarily American—of searching for offshore deposits of hydrocarbons in ever more demanding terrain resides primarily with the companies. "You've seen it happen already in Asia," the head of explorations for one middle-sized American firm stated in 1973. "Burma, India, the Philippines, and to a certain extent Japan and Pakistan, all tried to find offshore oil on their own. Now they have to turn to us. . . ." In addition, in the longer term, the overwhelming percentage of the great sums sure to be expended on alternate energy forms by the U.S., Europe, and Japan will gravitate toward those multinational energy facilitators once mundanely known as oil companies. [p. 18]

But this grand scheme for monopolizing world energy *depends on high oil prices*. Without them the development of offshore oil, oil shale, coal on a massive scale, etc., does not get off the drawing boards. These sources can only be made profitable at higher world energy prices.

At the same time the simultaneous inflationary boom of the advanced capitalist countries in 1972–73, primed by deficit spending and massive credit expansion in all of the leading capitalist powers, created an irresistible demand for oil at higher prices. In this context OPEC raised its prices. The oil-producing nations did not create the inflation; they responded to it.

Nor did Washington oppose the OPEC move. On the contrary, the oil trusts greedily utilized it to escalate other aspects of their world energy plan, especially the rolling back of U.S. environmental laws in order to build the trans-Alaska pipeline and develop offshore oil.

Since the Western oil companies control the oil industry "downstream," that is, the piping, refining, and marketing of petroleum, they were able to pass on price rises to consumers, no doubt lifting prices even more in the process. And it is sometimes forgotten that the raising of world prices allowed the oil industry to charge higher prices for *domestically produced oil,* which remains the major source of the oil consumed in the United States, the world's largest market for oil. This point was confirmed by the U.S. government itself at a forum at Yale University in late November 1974. The government representative was Thomas O. Enders, Assistant Secretary of State for Economic and Business Affairs. Enders "is regarded by insiders as the chief architect of Secretary of State Kissinger's energy policy" according to *New York Times* expert Leonard Silk (November 27, 1974).

"The startling news broken by Mr. Enders at Yale," Silk wrote, "startling against the background of repeated declarations of high American officials that OPEC nations must reduce their exorbitantly high prices—is that the United States is now founding its strategy on the $11 price."

Enders explained that such a high price was necessary to protect "heavy American and other Western investment in the development of alternative energy sources, based on the assumption of a continued 'real' oil price of $11 a barrel."

Enders even went so far as to explain that if the United States succeeds in driving down the price of world oil (in order to weaken the oil position of OPEC countries) the oil trusts would still favor a higher oil price in the imperialist countries themselves—a "two tier" world oil price system. "In other words," Leonard Silk said, "if the world oil price dropped to $5 a barrel before the Western oil coalition—which might be considered anti-OPEC—was ready, the United States and its partners would continue to pay $11 to their domestic producers.

"Foreign oil would then enter this country only at about the $11 price, with the United States Government collecting the $6 difference, whether via a tariff, through a Governmental oil-importing agency, or some other device. The foreign oil would be sold to domestic distributors at a price that would not shake current domestic investment in future energy development."

To top it off, the oil industries deduct their royalties to foreign governments from U.S. income taxes. The resulting historic profits are well known.

This much the energy trusts clearly foresaw and welcomed. They had another central objective: to weaken their rivals in Europe and Japan.

It is easy to forget that not so many years ago, as Japanese textiles, steel, autos, and electrical equipment carved out larger and larger sections of the U.S. market, there was much talk about the "Japanese miracle" and the soon-to-be "Japanese superpower." The Nixon administration labored for months to get an agreement from Tokyo to reduce textile exports and to accept quotas on steel to be shipped to the United States. But in one sweeping gesture Japanese capitalism was brought to its knees. It must import 99.3 percent of the oil it consumes. Eighty percent of this oil is controlled by the U.S.-dominated oil majors.

In Europe the effects were also devastating. So far as the October war itself was concerned, an attempt by the European powers to prevent Washington from using their military bases did not even bring the Secretary of State to the telephone. U.S. arms were rushed to Israel via bases in the Azores. The two actual superpowers armed and financed the adversaries and settled the war in secret.

"The year of the European Economic Community's auspicious enlargement to include Britain and put it on the world map ended in the frustrations of failure to cohere on any urgent issue," the previously cited Institute for Strategic Studies 1973 survey declared. "By the end of the year some serious observers even wondered if it might not be disintegrating. Attempts to achieve European monetary union, with Britain, Italy and (in January 1974) France all floating their currencies, left a kind of Deutschmark zone as the rump of monetary Europe; West Germany became increasingly restless at footing Community bills, and over the oil crisis Britain and France played lone hands to the point where Chancellor Brandt remarked that 'if we do not stand united . . . we shall not realize anything lasting'" (p. 5).

How Much Development Can Petrodollars Buy?
The Case of Iran

A deeply divided world imperialism now faces an entirely unprecedented phenomenon: subalterns with two things the imperialists desperately want—oil and money. If we can dismiss the contention that the OPEC governments are holding the world to ransom or were the unilateral cause of skyrocketing oil prices, there remains to be considered the very real impact of the infusion of literally tens of billions of dollars into nations that have barely emerged from medieval backwardness. Is a great leap forward into industrialism and even a new Middle Eastern imperialism in the offing, or will the backward social structures of these countries dissipate and devalue the potential effects of such a vast capital accumulation fund? There are several reasons why Iran provides the best test of the effect of petrodollars in the region.

Iran has the largest population of any Middle Eastern country after Egypt and Turkey. Unlike them, however, it has massive oil reserves, the third largest in the world after Saudi Arabia and Kuwait. Here is a list of the major financial deals that Iran concluded or was negotiating as of September 1974 as compiled from the *Middle East Economic Digest:*

For the exploration and development of onshore oil, the National Iranian Oil Corporation (NIOC) entered into separate agreements with Deminex (Deutsche Erdoelversorgungsgesellschaft—Germany), Compagnie Française des Pétroles (CFP—France), Ultramar (Britain), Ashland Oil (U.S.), and Pan-Canadian Petroleum. In these agreements the Western firms supply the technology and personnel, but the oil, once developed, reverts to NIOC.

For the development and production of offshore gas in one of the world's biggest gas fields, a consortium has been formed: Kalingas (Kangan Liquefied Natural Gas), composed of Nissho-Iwai (Japan), International Systems and Control Corp. (U.S.), Chicago Bridge and Iron (U.S.), Simonsen and Astrup (ships, Norway), and National Iranian Gas.

For development and production of onshore gas in the same region, believed to hold 175,000 billion cubic feet, another consortium: Egoco, composed of Elf-ERAP (France, 32 percent), ENI (Italy, 28 percent), Hispanoil (Spain, 20 percent), Petrofina (Belgium, 15 percent), OMV (Austria, 5 percent).

For building refineries. A 500,000-barrel-a-day refinery with NIOC and the U.S. consortium Iran-American Refining and Marketing (Apco Oil, Cities Service, Clark Oil, Crown Central Petroleum); and with Japan, a $1 billion refinery and petrochemical plant.

Petro and other chemicals. CDF-Chimie (France) and the National Petrochemical Corporation of Iran (NPC), for a petrochemical complex; Dow Chemical Europe (U.S.) and NPC, a $500 million petrochemical and plastic plant to produce on a 50-50 basis; Union Carbide (U.S.) and NPC, a $700 million jointly owned petrochemical complex (and an agreement whereby Iran acquires 20 percent participation in Union Carbide Caribe, a Union Carbide subsidiary); E.I. DuPont de Nemours (U.S.), 40 percent, and Iranian companies, 60 percent, a $250 million synthetic fibers plant (with later public sales of securities envisioned); and Sahu Jain (India) and NPC, a $250 million chemical complex for the production of ammonia and urea. Abroad, Iran, Japan, and Australia are considering the development of a petrochemical complex in the Pilbara region of northeast Australia.

Other oil-related developments. Elf-ERAP (France) and Technip (France) agreed to construct a $600 million gas liquefication plant; Gazocean (France) for the sale of twelve liquefied-gas tankers valued at $1.1 billion; St. Gobain-Pont-á-Mousson (France) and Gaz de France for a pipeline from Iran to Turkey valued at $600 million; Halfdan Ditlev-Simonsa (Norway) for twenty liquefied-gas tankers of 125,000 cubic meters each (about $120 million per ship). And abroad, NIOC and Italy's ENI have been negotiating an agreement which could see NIOC participation in AGIP-ENI, ENI's service station and refinery operations outside Italy. This agreement would include guaranteed oil imports to Italy.

For nuclear power, France has agreed to build five stations with a 1,000 megawatt capacity each, due to be completed in 1985 at a cost of about $1.3 billion. The United States has negotiated to build two nuclear reactors plus supplying the enriched uranium for them. West Germany is to build a 600 megawatt nuclear power plant.

"In one industry, steel," reported the September 20, 1974, *Middle East Economic Digest,* "the Government is planning to raise production from the present level of about 600,000 tons to 15 million tons a year by 1982. . . . The plans are in the hands of the Iranian Steel Industries Corporation . . . already advancing rapidly towards the implementation of projects which the corporation's Chairman, Reza Amin, told *MEED* will involve investment around $2,000 million from foreign and private sources. . . . The projects include a three million-tons-a-year plant to be set up at Bandar Abbas by Finsider of Italy. . . . Thysen of West Germany is to set up a plant at Ahwaz . . . and Korf will set up another plant. . . . Cruesot Loire of France is to set up a special steel mill. . . . The British Steel Corporation has also reached initial agreement on setting up a cold rolling mill at Isfahan."

These are all business enterprises of the first magnitude. And to this list must be added Iran's foreign investments, most notably its $100 million purchase in July of 25.04 percent of West Germany's giant Friederich Krupp Huettenwerke, the implications of which will be discussed later.

If money alone can end underdevelopment, no country in the world could ever hope for a better opportunity to buy its way into the modern age. And much rides on the outcome of this test. Can capitalism promise a way out of poverty in the former colonial world, at least in those countries fortunate enough to get a corner on a relatively scarce natural resource? At the least, does it mean that Iran and the Arab oil-producing states will shortly cease to be semicolonial nations and join the ranks of the lesser imperialist powers, perhaps as "subimperialisms"? And if this last were so, would it not mean that socialists would no longer be under any obligation to side with them in any future conflicts with Washington, inasmuch as this would have become a mere interimperialist rivalry and no longer a clash between oppressed and oppressor nations?

The whole weight of official propaganda in the United States and Europe aims at pushing the working class and its political representatives into renouncing defense of the Arab and Iranian states against foreign capital.

The *New York Times* in an editorial December 1, 1974, says that "the kind of minimal measures the United States has taken thus far cannot break the world oil cartel or stanch the massive transfer of money—and power—to the Middle East."

The *Christian Science Monitor* stated November 7, 1974: "Saudi Arabia has zoomed to the rank of fourth richest nation in the world and soon will surpass all but West Germany in foreign-exchange reserves, as the massive transfer of wealth to oil producing and exporting countries moves into high gear."

Iran is singled out for even more virulent propaganda of this character. "The Shah," *Time* magazine declared November 4, 1974, "is determined to transform Iran . . . into a Middle Eastern superpower."

Fortune magazine carried an article in its October 1974 issue entitled, "The Shah Drives to Build a New Persian Empire." "Among the Middle Eastern countries inundated with oil wealth," wrote *Fortune* author Louis Kraar, "a non-Arab nation, Iran, seems to be in the most favorable position of all. . . .

"The Shah believes that the Western powers have entered a long period of decline. Sitting on the richly carpeted veranda of Ramsar Palace, he told me that democratic governments have been undermined by 'permissiveness'. . . . One reason the easy life has been possible, he says, is that the industrial countries have coasted along on cheap oil at Iran's expense.

"As the most dramatic part of his bid for imperial power and prestige, the Shah intends to make the kingdom's military forces among the most awesome in the world."

It is obvious that these words have been carefully chosen by the editors to help foster a climate in which the "democratic" United States can intervene to beat back the regimes in Teheran, Raiydh, Damascus, etc., if a situation favorable to the imperialists presents itself. For that reason it is of the utmost importance that theoretical clarity be maintained in evaluating both the extent *and the limits* of the effects of the flood of petrodollars into the Middle East.

What are the fundamental relations between imperialist and semicolonial countries? To what extent can or have these been altered by the new wealth of the Middle East? To put these questions on a scientific basis it is most helpful to turn to Lenin's *Imperialism* (1916). Although much has happened since Lenin wrote this pamphlet to explain the central causes of World War I, the framework set forth by Lenin allows a rational discussion of the question far removed from the demagogic outpourings of the editorial offices of New York's leading bourgeois newspapers and magazines.

For Lenin the distinguishing feature of imperialism is *finance capital.* As a Marxist category, Lenin uses "finance capital" to describe not only the various economic forms capital takes in leading industrial powers (the merger of industrial capital with banking and other forms of money capital) but also to describe the social relations lying behind these economic forms. Lenin wrote, "It is characteristic of capitalism in general that the ownership of capital is separated from the application of capital to production, that money capital is separated from industrial or productive capital, and that the rentier, who lives entirely on income obtained from money capital, is separated from the entrepreneur and from all who are directly concerned in the management of capital. Imperialism, or the domination of finance capital, is that highest stage of capitalism in which this separation reaches vast proportions. The supremacy of finance capital over all other forms of capital means the predominance of the rentier and the financial oligarchy; it means the crystallisation of a small number of financially 'powerful' states from among all the rest" (p. 59).

Lenin stressed the role of finance capital in giving the

capitalist superpowers world domination: "Capitalism has grown into a world system of colonial oppression and of the financial strangulation of the overwhelming majority of the people of the world by a handful of 'advanced' countries. And this 'booty' is shared between two or three powerful world marauders armed to the teeth (America, Great Britain, Japan), who involve the world in *their* war over the sharing of *their* booty" (pp. 10-11).

Lenin emphasized that even those transitional semicolonial countries that were politically independent of the superpowers remained subordinate to them:

"It must be observed that finance capital and its corresponding foreign policy, which reduces itself to the struggle of the Great Powers for economic and political division of the world, give rise to a number of *transitional* forms of national dependence. The division of the world into two main groups—of colony-owning countries on the one hand and colonies on the other—is not the only typical feature of this period; there is also a variety of forms of dependent countries; countries which, officially, are politically independent, but which are, in fact, enmeshed in the net of financial and diplomatic dependence" (p. 85).

It is true that certain factors, both long-term and conjunctural, have offered a number of dependent regimes in the former colonial world a greater room for maneuver than in the past. These include the emergence of noncapitalist societies, from the Soviet Union to Cuba; the weakening of the old colonial powers in World War II; the rise of socialist or nationalist revolutionary movements in the semicolonial countries; and, more recently, the weakening of American imperialism as a result of the setback suffered in Southeast Asia, the rise of a new radicalism in the U.S., and the intensification of interimperialist competition. This has permitted not only some Middle Eastern governments but also some Latin American and Asian ones to renegotiate the terms of their dependence and capture a marginally larger share of the profits extracted from their countries' natural resources and cheap labor.

It is a mistake, however, to confine examination of this development to its purely "financial" aspects. The historical resultants must be taken into consideration: the unbridgeable gap between the semicolonial capitalist nations and the vast technical, cultural, and military apparatus of the advanced capitalist countries, the "powerful world marauders armed to the teeth" described by Lenin. Neither membership in that exclusive club nor "autonomy" from it can be secured today by the mere accumulation of capital, however imposing the sums involved.

The financial subordination of the semicolonies to imperialism has not fundamentally changed. Imperialist monopoly remains the yoke that holds the majority of the world's population under conditions of permanent impoverishment, if not outright starvation. One example, taken from among many, should help to illustrate this.

The spokesmen for OPEC have justified their price increases on the ground of the long-term price differentials between raw materials, their main export, and the food and finished products that the semicolonial world must buy back from the imperialists. They are correct in this. Even with their radical investment proposals, the semicolonial nations of the Middle East do not have any serious prospect of fundamentally altering the exploitative effects of the trade differential because they will have to import all of their technology, finished plants, experts, finished goods, and substantial amounts of food from the imperialist metropolises.

In this respect it cannot be stressed too heavily that while imperialist propaganda complains about the supposedly devastating effect of higher oil prices on advanced capitalist countries, tens of millions of people are starving in underdeveloped countries *because the United States is charging higher prices for food, of which it is the main exporter, on world markets.*

While the U.S. oil trusts favor high oil prices and had already taken steps to force prices upwards long before October 1973, they do not favor nationalization or participation agreements in any form. They would prefer to own the oil from the ground to the gas pump *and there is a real danger that they will go to war to reassert this "right."*

The five distinguishing features of imperialism that Lenin gives in his pamphlet still hold. Lenin said:

Without forgetting the conditional and relative value of all definitions, which can never include all the concatenations of a phenomenon in its complete development, we must give a definition of imperialism that will embrace the following five essential features:

1) The concentration of production and capital developed to such a high stage that it created monopolies which play a decisive role in economic life.

2) The merging of bank capital with industrial capital, and the creation, on the basis of this "finance capital," of a "financial oligarchy."

3) The export of capital, which has become extremely important, as distinguished from the export of commodities.

4) The formation of international capitalist monopolies which share the world among themselves.

5) The territorial division of the whole world among the greatest capitalist powers. . . . [p. 89]

To what extent do the governments of the Middle East display these distinguishing traits? Let us return to the case of Iran.

Iran: A Billionaire Pauper?

Iran offers the best case because it has the combination of a large population and oil reserves. Let us attempt an initial projection of Iran's possibilities as a "future Middle East superpower," as *Time* called it, on the basis of Lenin's five characteristics of imperialism.

We have already caught a glimpse of the kind of industrial development that is in store for Iran. This is overwhelmingly devoted to oil, gas, and petrochemical production. Where there were suggestions a year ago that Iran would go slow on the use of its petroleum reserves, the orientation now seems to be to get the oil out of the ground as fast as possible and sell it while high royalties still prevail. (For reasons which will be taken up later, there is little expectation that the present level of royalties will stick for the decade.)

In its present five-year plan the Iranian government projects a gigantic 51.5 percent a year growth in oil and gas production which it hopes will bring the GNP up to $54.6 billion in 1978.

But the gross figures, if realized, are deceptive. There will not be an across-the-board industrialization that will bring jobs and income to the great mass of the Iranian people. The industrial projects already announced are overwhelmingly capital-intensive and export-oriented, such as petrochemicals and steel (which will actually still require the import of foreign skilled labor). This is a formula for an extremely lopsided development, leaving intact the backward social structures of traditional precapitalist society. The thoroughly inadequate proposals for agrarian reform are a signal indicator of the limitations of such a grafting on of industrialism from the top in the age of imperialism.

In fact, to an important extent, the shah's promise to develop "his" country—the much-touted "White Revolution"—is public relations fakery. Frances FitzGerald reminds us of the social realities in Iran in *Harper's Magazine* (November 1974):

In Teheran two-thirds of all families have an income of $200 per person per year. . . . In the rural areas, where 58 percent of the population still live, over a third of all families earn less than $400 a year, while another 40 percent earn less than $800, and the inflation rate this year is 18 to 20 percent. . . . In the countryside there is widespread malnutrition—an average calorie intake in Iran is about the same as India's—and the rural people suffer from all the diseases that come with such conditions. About 70 percent of Iranians are illiterate (the government Statistics Center says 63 percent, and the Shah says 75 percent when he wants to emphasize the necessity for authoritarian rule). There are only 9,500 practicing physicians in the country—or one for every 3,300 people. Nearly half of them live in Teheran, and a great percentage of these cater only to the rich. . . . Each year half the medical-school graduates leave the country—there are more Iranian doctors in New York than there are in any city outside Teheran. The phrase "brain drain" was coined in Iran. In other words, despite its oil money and vaunted government stability, Iran is basically worse off than a country like Syria that has had neither—and a war going on—for the past twenty-five years.

There is no small amount of propaganda implicit in the government figures on industrial production cited before. An example is the projection of 15 million tons of steel production by 1982. That is fully one-tenth of the steel produced in peak years in the United States. It is announced at a time of recurring glut in world steel markets, of intensive competition, and drastic concentration and centralization of the mightiest U.S., European, and Japanese steel combines. One must take with considerable skepticism the prospect of successful entry of Iran into this market in the near future.

The real monopolies operating in the Middle East, however, are not the home-grown creation of the oil billionaires but the well-established Western "multinational" corporations which, as could be seen from the list above, have an interest of their own in virtually all of the industrialization projects so far contemplated.

The imperialist powers are scrambling for the new wealth of the Middle East. *Business Week* noted November 23, 1974:

The four U.S. oil giants who are partners in the Arabian American Oil Co. (Aramco) are getting set to start new operations in Saudi Arabia just at a time when the Saudis are about to take over their remaining [40 percent] share of the company. The apparent paradox has a simple explanation: The oil companies want to bid on some of the billions of dollars' worth of contracts that the Saudis will hand out. . . .

The same motive that spurs the Aramco quartet—Exxon, Texaco,

Socal, and Mobil—is luring hordes of other eager businessmen to Saudi Arabia. By the middle of next year, the Saudis will have a five-year economic development plan that will include a shopping list for at least $70-billion worth of goods, services, and technology.

This process is depicted as a telescoped example of primitive accumulation of national capital that will enable full-scale industrial development in the near future. But in the absence of a monopoly of foreign trade to exclude cheaper manufactured goods—and the military means to enforce it—which can be achieved only through a socialized planned economy, fools and their money will soon be parted. The production and trade agreements between imperialism and the Middle East will more closely bind the economies and policies of these countries to the advanced capitalist powers of the West.

Comparison with a previous historical example of the sudden accumulation of vast wealth, the California gold rush of 1848, provides some insights into the present process in the Middle East. That scramble for riches put California on the capitalist map, ultimately making it a leading industrial center in the U.S. and world markets. But this took place within the boundaries of one of the most advanced nations of its day, in a militarily unassailable part of the world, and with great untapped markets yet to be opened. But this is no longer 1848. None of these conditions apply to the Middle East. And it should be added that even today, the California industrialists have yet to come close to matching the economic power of their counterparts in the Eastern section of the United States whose financial empires have roots going back a century earlier, to prerevolutionary American capital formations.

The American and European brigands doing secret business in Teheran already command world empires. Their intention is to bring Iranian and Arab monopoly under their control, not to give it a free hand to develop independently.

Banking Capital

Even if we narrow our focus to the category of banking capital—in this case primarily petrodollar reserves—the subordination of the Middle East to imperialism remains clear.

We have already seen that the large reserves of petrodollars are actually held in Western currencies or bank deposits, especially in the United States and Britain. This not only expresses a subordination of these moneys to the economies of the imperialist nations *but also to their state power.* Both Western and Arab and Iranian financiers are fully aware of this and can even speak in public of the ease with which these or other assets could be frozen. Republican Senator Charles Percy, a former banker himself, read into the *Congressional Record* November 20, 1974, an article he had written in the *American Banker.* The OPEC countries, said Percy, "have preferred the liquidity and anonymity of short term deposits over long term investments. The desire for anonymity probably reflects a fear that the industrialized nations might freeze their accounts for political leverage to bargain prices down." It is one reason they are so cautious in their foreign investment policies. And this clearly expresses a relation between money capitals that is completely uneven.

But there is further chicanery involved in the imperialist pretense that the Arab- and Iranian-owned petrodollar reserves constitute some kind of super capital holding. Recall the suggestion of *Newsweek* magazine that reserves of $35 billion in Saudi Arabia could make it the world's leading financial power— "by this measurement," they admitted. But it is precisely this measurement that conceals the actual relationship of forces.

Because there is no significant development of industrial monopoly in these countries, because they do not have *real* finance capital, and because there is no "financial oligarchy" on anything like the scale of advanced capitalism, the capital of these nations is concentrated in the state treasury. And in these transitional forms of state capitalist economies the state treasury plays a central role. It does not do this in imperialist powers. There the state treasury is entirely subordinate to the corporations. (The reserves of the United States, in fact, have hovered at the level of about $14 billion since 1968.)

If one wants to compare economies, it must be between Middle East treasuries and foreign *bank assets.* With this comparison, of course, the whole pretense of *Newsweek* falls apart. The assets of the three largest U.S. banks in 1973 were each larger than the projected figure for Saudi Arabia's treasury in 1975 (Bank of America, $49.4 billion; First National City, $44 billion; Chase Manhattan, $36 billion)! The combined assets of the fifty largest U.S. banks is $459 billion—and this is still strictly in the realm of banking capital.

Finance capital is an interpenetration of banking and industrial capital. To compare economies in *Imperialism,* Lenin used the total value of the financial securities of nations. In this respect a revealing basis of judgment is the total *U.S. debt*—that is, the actual claims that already exist on the U.S. economy, including industry, construction, and government. The *New York Times* rails that the "unspendable claims" of all OPEC countries next year will be $120 billion. But this year, the "unspendable claims" on the United States (that is, the U.S. debt) already stand at $2.5 trillion—over twenty times that amount. The U.S. debt is so great that it would take a sum more than one-third the gross national product of Japan just to pay this year's interest on it.

Arab and Iranian state capital is not in this league.

It is true that the gigantic pile of paper money may one day prove to be unredeemable. But when this happens and United States credit collapses—and this is the real potential crisis of world imperialism—it will express the long-run inability of imperialist capital to find productive investments on a world scale. It cannot be blamed on petrodollars.

The Export of Capital

Lenin's third category is the export of capital. Here again it is necessary to put figures in proportion. For reasons already discussed, little Arab and Iranian capital is flowing into productive investments abroad, the most spectacular case so far being the purchase of one-quarter of the Krupp steelworks. It remains to be seen whether this is the triumph of Arab cunning depicted in the Western press. That depends on how good a buy one quarter of Krupp is at $100 million (the most frequently cited figure).

In any event, $100 million would be sufficient to purchase only about 5 percent of the stock of United States Steel Corp., even at its presently quite depressed level. To purchase all the corporations listed on the New York Stock Exchange at 1973 average stock prices would have required $721 billion. This is inconceivable on political grounds—Washington has already turned down the shah's offer to purchase Grumman (the 156th largest U.S. corporation); and similar purchase attempts will run into similar political obstacles. But purchasing a major share of U.S. corporations is also inconceivable on financial grounds.

It would be a mistake in any case to examine the reciprocal foreign investments by U.S. and Arab financiers from the standpoint of a purely formal equality. U.S. foreign investments are secured by the untold economic and military might of the nuclear-armed American technological giant. Foreign investments of the Arab sheiks and the Iranian shah are protected by—

the willingness of the host government to recognize the legitimacy of the investment. On the one side there is actual power; on the other a mere legal "right" that can be canceled at will. This alone means that in the long run exported Arab and Iranian capital will be subordinate to the imperialist powers where the investments are made. The Middle Eastern governments cannot today look forward to rising above the status of junior partner on some of the boards of big imperialist monopolies.

Who Controls the Oil Business?

The subordinate role of Arab and Middle East industry to international monopoly (Lenin's fourth category) is evident *in the petroleum industry itself*. The OPEC countries have been unable to significantly weaken the world monopoly of the international petroleum cartel.

To convince everyone of the supposed Arab oil threat, the imperialists have concentrated on the present known reserves of oil. It should never be forgotten that practically all the information available on oil and other energy reserves comes from the oil companies themselves. But, leaving that aside, they have a point: 66 percent of measured petroleum reserves in the capitalist world exist in the Middle East.

This means that now and for a long time to come, the world will require Middle East oil.

But this oil is not consumed in the Middle East. Only a tiny fraction, less than one percent of world production of petroleum and gas, is consumed in these countries. It has to go abroad— "downstream"—and the Middle East nations and Iran do not own the downstream facilities. As of December 31, 1973, according to *The Oil and Gas Journal,* there were 31 refineries in the Middle East with a total crude capacity of 2.9 billion barrels per day. This compares to 714 refineries with a daily capacity of 53.5 billion barrels in the capitalist world as a whole, so that only 4.4 percent of the refineries and 5.2 percent of refining capacity exists in the Middle East. Most of the refineries in the capitalist world are still owned by the Western oil trusts.

The refinery-building projects underway in the Middle East today cannot significantly alter this equation.

Even more pronounced is the Western hold on tankers. The most recent complete list of figures available reported the number of vessels owned in 1971 by the fifteen largest tanker-owning countries. No Middle East countries are on this list. It has been seen that Iran projects purchasing some 32 tankers over the next few years. That would still not place it on the list; the smallest number of tankers in 1971 of the top fifteen was held by West Germany—60 tankers. Greece held 291; Norway, 373; Japan, 388; and Liberia, 777, according to the U.S. Department of the Interior *(Minerals in the World Economy,* p. 14).

The peculiar reasons why most U.S. shipping is conducted under the Liberian flag themselves testify to the "advantages" of being an imperialist power. The United States has developed its "special relations" with this African country for over a century. Further, concessions had to be wrung from American seamen in order for so much U.S. shipping to be done with foreign crews. (Most of these ships, of course, are owned by the U.S. oil trusts.) Can Iran, or even the Middle East as a whole, envision breaking this shipping monopoly?

In addition, the oil interests own all of the facilities for distributing oil and gas in the Western markets where it is overwhelmingly consumed.

All of these factors have made it possible for the oil trusts to absorb higher oil royalties and even substantially increase their profits while doing so. For one thing, the "energy crisis" strengthened the hand of the oil majors against the "independents." (In the United States it saw the wiping out of whole chains of service stations owned by "domestic" oil.)

In less guarded moments, spokesmen for the oil trusts admit as much. *New York Times* reporter William Smith was told by John Lichtblau, head of the Petroleum Industry Research Foundation, "The oil companies are being circumscribed, but they are willing to work under any conditions in which they can make money. By 1985 the companies will still be the major transporters, refiners and marketers of oil in the world" (July 7, 1974).

A salient proof of the inability of the OPEC countries to break the U.S. monopoly on world petroleum was the *failure of the 1973-74 boycott.* One has to acknowledge the success of imperialist propaganda in convincing most people that the Arab oil boycott worked and that a new one is a severe threat. But when it comes down to discussing serious questions, such as war strategy, the imperialists know better. The 1973 survey of the Institute for Strategic Studies explained as follows why the Arab oil boycott was lifted:

> First, it had become evident that, as Dr. Pachachi has foreseen, the embargoes on the United States and the Netherlands were not ca-

pable of being effectively applied. There was enough non-Arab oil to permit elaborate switches of supplies by the oil companies, so that all their customers were in effect rationed equally. . . . Second, when it became evident that the embargo was not working and that Europe and Japan were pliable, the Arabs had little to gain and much to lose by precipitating a major recession in the industrial world. [p. 33]

The Arab boycott failed because it ran up against the superior power of U.S. imperialism. To the extent that the Arabs did attempt to exploit interimperialist rivalry, they failed, according to these experts, because of the weakness of Europe and Japan in this rivalry. The U.S. was unhurt by the boycott; Europe and Japan were hurt but incapable of compelling Washington to do anything about it.

Perhaps the most dramatic testimony of all to the power of international monopoly, however, is not the hold the oil trusts presently have on world oil, but their plans for the future. They are scouring the globe to discover and develop alternate sources of oil and other energy forms. Oil fields are being opened from the Arctic to the South China Sea.

Politically the oil companies have launched a massive propaganda offensive, not only to blame the Arabs and Iran for their problems, but to pave the way for exploiting the huge coal, offshore oil, and oil-shale reserves of the North American continent.

Millions of dollars are pumped into foundations and "think tanks" to come up with long-range plans for energy conservation and development. Quite out of keeping with the claim that the United States is about to run out of oil were figures published by the "Energy Policy Project" of the Ford Foundation in October 1974. This two-year, $4 million inquiry into energy concluded that "the U.S. can balance its energy budget, control pollution, and avoid reliance on insecure oil sources abroad by slowing its growth rate on energy consumption." The interesting figures are tables calculating the *undiscovered recoverable resources* in the United States and Alaska. Including both onshore and offshore oil, the Ford Foundation believes there are 200-400 billion barrels of undiscovered recoverable petroleum here in addition to what is already known. The upper figure exceeds the entire known reserves of the Middle East. The figure for undiscovered recoverable natural gas is 1,000 to 2,000 trillion cubic feet. For oil shale the study shows 418 billion identified and 800 billion undiscovered barrels where the oil shale yield is 25 to 100 gallons per ton; in the 10 to 25 gallons per ton category, the identified deposits move up to 1,600 billion barrels and the undiscovered, to 25,000 billion barrels; and in the 5 to 10 gallons per ton category, the figures are 2,200 billion barrels identified and 138,000 billion barrels undiscovered *(A Time to Choose,* pp. 477–84). The last figure runs to 400 times the known Middle Eastern reserves!

Of course the present technology is far from being able to exploit such low-yield oil-shale reserves at a profit.

What is important to grasp is that the imperialist oil trusts are striving, from Britain's North Sea to Prudhoe Bay in Alaska, *to break the Mideast monopoly on reserves.* And there can be little doubt that over the next decade they will do this, whether or not they have gone to war in the meantime. This is why the Arab and Iranian planners themselves do not count on permanent high royalties. The price of world oil must remain high. But the Middle East countries will not be able to maintain their present high shares of the take on these prices. (And this, in turn, is one of the reasons that the Arab and Iranian governments are pressing for the highest possible royalties now. Mana Saeed al-Otaiba, petroleum minister of the United Arab Emirates, said in Beirut in November 1974: "These profits [of the Western companies] are being used by them to find alternative sources for our oil. They are investing on a huge scale in the Arctic and the North Sea. Our wealth is being squeezed, and piled-up profits are being used to do away with our oil. . . . This we will not accept.")

As important as Arab and Iranian nationalized oil has now become, it is not on a par with the international petroleum cartel. Precisely because the latter *is* an international monopoly, it can undertake the colossal revolutionization of world energy production that is presently underway.

Military Dependency

The United States role of policing world imperialism goes beyond anything envisioned by Lenin when he discussed the territorial division of the world among superpowers. Washington will spend more on its military apparatus this year than all OPEC nations will realize in oil profits. Europe and Japan depend on the U.S. military machine to defend capitalism in their own territory in the final analysis; and every semicolonial country is penetrated to one degree or another by the U.S. war and intelligence apparatus.

In wars, the policies of the United States and the Soviet Union are by far the most decisive among the existing governments. This is well known in the Middle East. Iran, especially, is developing a military policy that is tailored to impress the Pentagon. Frances FitzGerald wrote in her *Harper's* article:

> The Pentagon has not released much information on the equipment sold, but it is known that last year Iran had outstanding orders for more than 200 F-4E and F-5E fighter aircraft, and nearly 600 helicopters. Iran also ordered 800 Chieftain main tanks and 250 Scorpion light tanks from Britain [which would be more than Britain's army has—D.R.]. This year Iran has bought 80 of the new Grumman long-range fighter-bombers, the F-14s. It has also bought the most advanced small missiles and so-called smart bombs that are guided by lasers or television devices. Iran has one of the largest helicopter fleets in the world. Until it was discovered that American defense contractors cannot sell shares to foreign countries, the Shah had considered buying Grumman. As it is, he is thought to be negotiating for the YF-16 and YF-17, two models of fighter-bombers that are still under development. With the addition of these aircraft he may well have the third-largest airforce in the world. In a few years Iran will have the capacity to manufacture an atom bomb, and by then, it will have a delivery system that can reach all the way to Moscow.

The purchase of weapons from Britain, France, and the United States increases the dependency of the purchaser on these powers. For when war breaks out, as the October war showed, the purchase of ammunition and other weapons does not stop. It increases. As large as the Middle Eastern military machines are becoming, their stocks cannot support a protracted war.

Time magazine said, November 4, 1974, "The Defense Department is pleased with the Shah's massive purchase of sophisticated U.S. weapons, but some intelligence analysts cynically regard the Shah as little more than America's hired gun in the Middle East."

Fortune noted in its October 1974 issue that Iran already "has used force to occupy three small disputed islands formerly held by a couple of miniature Arab Gulf states, and it has 1,300 soldiers with helicopters helping nearby Oman quell a band of Marxist-led rebels."

At home, the shah's notorious police force, undoubtedly working closely with the CIA, terrorizes the population. FitzGerald wrote:

> The secret police, called by its Persian acronym, SAVAK, has agents in the lobby of every hotel, in every government department, and in

every university classroom. In the provinces, the SAVAK runs a political intelligence-gathering service, and abroad it keeps a check on every Iranian student. Private estimates put the number of SA-VAK agents at 70,000. . . . Educated Iranians cannot trust anyone beyond a close circle of friends. . . . The SAVAK intensifies this fear by giving no account of its activities. People simply disappear in Iran, and their disappearances go unrecorded. . . . The Shah says that his government has no political prisoners (Communists, he explains, are not political offenders but common criminals). Amnesty International estimates that there are about 20,000 of them.

To what extent does Iran enter into the Pentagon's military policies beyond the Middle East? This is hard to determine so far. There are hints that a role is envisioned for Iran in policing the Indian Ocean, an area of increasing strategic importance in Washington's encirclement of the Soviet Union. Surely, if Iran is building missiles with the capacity of striking Moscow, these are subordinate to the Pentagon's own contingency plans for World War III. Iran is not going to take Moscow on alone!

The Centrality of U.S. Imperialism

What we have attempted to describe is the centrality of U.S. imperialism in world oil politics and the secondary place of the Middle East governments, in relation not only to the United States, but to the other imperialist powers as well. The billions in oil revenues will not change this.

This does not mean that there is a harmony of interests between Washington and the Middle Eastern ruling classes. While the sheiks and shahs depend ultimately on imperialist support for their survival, they are riding a wave of nationalist sentiment that compels them to make a show of independence from the United States. The inflow of vast fortunes also raises the level of expectations of the Arab and Iranian masses, which spells potentially explosive consequences. Caught between the hammer of imperialist demands and the anvil of mass resentment, these rulers may find themselves in the leadership of anti-imperialist struggles they neither expected nor sought.

A precise understanding of the extent and the limits of the effects of the petrodollar flood is crucial today to prepare the opponents of imperialism to meet the next great explosion in the Middle East in confident and united action in defense of the historically oppressed Arab and Iranian peoples.

The Decline of the
American Colossus

The two hundredth anniversary of the first American revolution coincides with a depression in the United States, the crumbling of Washington's puppet military dictatorships in Pnompenh and Saigon, and the first recession on a world scale since 1937-38.

Workers of every major capitalist country are suffering from a rise in unemployment. As 1974 ended, unemployment in Japan had soared by 40 percent in that one year to 750,000 or 1.5 percent of the labor force. Officially admitted rates were 3 percent in Britain, 3.3 percent in France, 4.2 percent in West Germany, and 8.2 percent in the United States. Across the "advanced" capitalist world at least 15 million workers were jobless and the number was rising daily.

There are disputes about applying the term "depression" to the U.S. downturn. In 1933, the worst year of the previous depression, national unemployment stood at slightly above 24 percent. Yet in February 1975 the unemployment rate in Detroit, the hardest-hit U.S. industrial center, already stood above 23 percent. For poor whites, youth, and Blacks in Detroit's inner city the jobless rate was above 50 percent. An unemployed Black Chrysler worker told a correspondent for *The Militant:* "Everything's poor man, really poor. I don't make but $134 every two weeks. . . . I expect to be unemployed forever."

A thousand miles to the southwest, in Albuquerque, New Mexico, an unemployed Chicano told a *New York Times* reporter: "I do not think I will be able to buy food stamps. It is too much." He and his wife and ten children live on $295 a month Social Security, $66 a month welfare, and $15 a month from a son who has a job. These are depression conditions. And every worker knows they are spreading.

It is too early to know whether massive government deficits will succeed in turning the American economy around in late 1975. That would stem the slide, at least within this particular business cycle, toward world economic collapse—although at the price of reintensified inflation. But it is now clear in any case that a turning point has been reached in international capitalism. The long-term, relatively crisis-free expansion of the post–World War II period is over. Increasingly frequent recessions, tending more and more to coincide in all capitalist countries and to be accompanied by accelerating inflation, are the order of the day.

In the United States the depression is spurring on the massive loss of confidence in the government, triggered by the slaughter in Southeast Asia and the lies surrounding it, by the Watergate exposures, and by the more recently disclosed activities of the CIA and FBI in the U.S. and abroad.

This is a historic crisis of legitimacy for U.S. imperialism. Politicians talk about the need for a "new consensus" or a "new sense of national unity," which they hope will make their domestic and foreign policies easier to sell to the workers who vote them into office. The more farsighted apologists recognize that there are no easy solutions. Some go so far as to propose that it is the ideological framework itself that needs to be overhauled. An example of this is offered by *Fortune* magazine, the business publication of Time-Life, Inc. For its special April 1975 issue, purporting to celebrate the bicentennial of the American revolution, *Fortune* assembled twelve authors and President Ford himself to discuss the excruciating problems facing American capitalism as it prepares to enter its third century. The issue is entitled "The American System." A more accurate title would be "In Defense of Capitalism in its Decline."

"Rising Expectations"

The basic view of the *Fortune* authors about the nature of the developing social crisis—although reached through fallacious reasoning and used to justify utterly reactionary conclusions—is correct. Briefly put, they contend: The advances the U.S. economy was able to attain for its citizens, especially in the first two decades after World War II, can no longer be achieved on anywhere near the same scale. And a serious political threat to the capitalist system flows from this contradiction between what the system can deliver and what people think it should deliver.

The *Fortune* authors spell out this theme as it pertains to every major social aspect of the capitalist system at home. "Raising expectations is a serious matter," says President Ford. "Setting a goal for the total ending of segregation by a certain date is raising an expectation which you cannot necessarily achieve."

Fortune economist Edmund Faltermayer writes: "Between 1945 and 1974, half of America's families moved into newly built houses, and the number of private automobiles on the road increased more than three times as fast as the population. In the heady atmosphere of all that prosperity, there seemed little doubt that further gains were merely a question of time.

"That golden assumption no longer looks so certain. . . .

"Future gains will not come as easily as those of the recent past."

Daniel Bell, one of the best-known American sociologists, is *Fortune*'s most pessimistic contributor: "The promise of plenty has been transformed into a revolution of rising expectations. . . .

"Just about *all* grievances now get dumped into the lap of government. . . .

"The direction of events is clear: the government has made a commitment, not only to create a substantial welfare state, *but to redress all economic and social inequalities as well.* And the commitment is largely irreversible. . . .

"The ultimate problem presented by the revolution of rising entitlements is not that it will cost a lot of money—although it will certainly do that. What is potentially more dangerous is the threat that the revolution presents to our political system. It threatens to overload the system, to confront it with far more grievances than legislators and judges know how to cope with" (emphasis in the original).

These concerns are well founded. There *are* growing expectations and dissatisfactions among millions of Americans. Modern technology can produce nuclear weapons and send rockets to the moon with minute precision but consumer goods are neither durable nor safe. Why do people have to live in shabby housing and crowded tenement slums? Why do the trains, buses, and subways work less and charge more? If Washington can spend hundreds of billions of dollars on weapons for its global military system, why aren't there enough jobs in the United States? Why isn't education and medical care free? What Bell arrogantly labels as "hedonistic" are the perfectly just demands of people for decent and fulfilling lives.

On top of this the capitalist government faces a further layer of contradictions. The democratic pretensions and promises that it refuses to carry out stand in stark contrast to the private privileges of the ruling class and the profit-making corporations that the government serves and defends. George Novack, a leading Marxist writer, treated this subject in depth in *Democracy and Revolution*, a 1971 book whose timeliness is increasing.

"A system in which the people do not control the most important decisions and actions of the government, their economy, their welfare or the course of their lives," says Novack, "can hardly be considered genuinely democratic. It can be more precisely defined as a plutocracy dressed in democratic disguise" (p. 199).

Novack notes that this same opinion was expressed by C. Wright Mills in *The Sociological Imagination* (1959): "The United States today I should say is generally democratic mainly in form and in the rhetoric of expectation." Bourgeois sociologist Bell has taken his time in recognizing the floodtide of rising expectations among the masses and its latent potential to capsize the capitalist ship of state.

Tortured Reasoning

Bell and his colleagues are obligated to come up with reasons why American capitalism can no longer deliver on the scale of the 1950s and 1960s. These reasons must cover up both the profit drive of the monopolies and the role of the ruling class which owns them. Not surprisingly they attempt to shift the blame from the decaying profit system to the oppressed and exploited victims of that system: the people at home and abroad are demanding "too much."

There is a supposedly inseparable link between rising expectations and inflation. The people make demands on the government that the government can meet only through massive expenditures and ultimately through deficits that cause inflation. But the only way to end inflation at this juncture is through massive unemployment. Thus rising expectations, inflation and unemployment, so the argument goes, are linked in a vicious circle that must result in economic crises.

(For an earlier and more detailed presentation of this thesis see *Inflation, A World-Wide Disaster* by Irving S. Friedman [New York: Houghton Mifflin, 1973]. Friedman, who is a top monetary expert in the United States, having served the government, the International Monetary Fund, the World Bank, and now the First

National City Bank, extends the argument that rising expectations cause inflation on a world scale, including in semicolonial nations.)

"Paradoxically," says Bell, "economic growth may be a source of a distinctive 'contradiction' of capitalism—a contradiction that may prove to be its undoing. For growth has become inextricably linked with inflation, and it seems unlikely that any democratic society can abolish inflation without disastrous political consequences.

"It is not as though Americans look upon inflation without concern; every survey taken in the last few years shows that inflation is an object of profound fear. . . . And yet every imaginable anti-inflationary policy impinges on the welfare of some major interest group. The simple fact is that no one wants to pay the price of ending inflation, and modern democratic governments [in fact, capitalist governments in general—D.R.] find it politically difficult to make any sizable group pay the bill."

The ultimate logic of this tortured argument is to blame the poor and elderly for inflation and even depression. *Fortune* economist Faltermayer carries the argument that far: "The country is heading for an unpleasant face-off between those who are getting angry about Social Security deductions and the elderly. . . . The utopian era of comfortable retirement wholly at government expense will have to be postponed indefinitely." The millions of poor elderly citizens who eke out bleak starvation-level existences in the slums of American cities or their retirement hovels will have the last say on this.

It is true that in the postwar epoch, capitalist growth and inflation are inextricably linked. But that can't be blamed on the relatively paltry outlays for social welfare made by the government. It has to do with fundamental contradictions of the capitalist system that the *Fortune* authors themselves do not treat. But if these contradictions are introduced into the discussion, they underline all the more the deepgoing character of the crisis *Fortune*'s bourgeois ideologues are seeking to allay.

Crisis

The insuperable contradiction of capitalist production, as Marx explained it, is that *growth itself leads to crisis.* The drive to accumulate capital is not linked to the needs of society, but solely to the profit needs of the owners of capital. "Fanatically bent on making value expand itself," Marx wrote in the first volume of

Capital, "[the capitalist] ruthlessly forces the human race to produce for production's sake. . . . The development of capitalist production makes it constantly necessary to keep increasing the amount of capital laid out in a given industrial undertaking, and competition makes the immanent laws of capitalist production to be felt by each individual capitalist, as external coercive laws. It compels him to keep constantly extending his capital, in order to preserve it, but extend it he cannot except by means of progressive accumulation. . . .

"Accumulate, accumulate! That is Moses and the prophets!" (pp. 492, 495).

The profit needs of capital periodically drive accumulation beyond the point where investments can, in fact, be profitably made. In 1899 Rosa Luxemburg wrote *Reform or Revolution*, a polemic against the "reformists" led by Eduard Bernstein in the German Social Democratic Party, who believed that capitalism could peacefully transform itself into a crisis-free system. If that could happen, she contended, it would mean "one of two things: either the world market can spread unlimitedly, or on the contrary the development of the productive forces is so fettered that it cannot pass beyond the bounds of the market. The first hypothesis constitutes a material impossibility. The second is rendered just as impossible by the constant technical progress that daily creates new productive forces in all branches" (p. 46).

Luxemburg's position is far from having been invalidated by subsequent history. Within less than two decades imperialism had plunged into the world war that she believed to be inevitable. Subsequently the expansionary drive of capital brought the Great Depression of the 1930s and a second interimperialist world war that dwarfed any horrors of capitalism that Marx saw. Imperialism's counterrevolutionary drive to suppress struggles for national liberation in order to control the semicolonies, especially their sources of raw materials, has not let up even for one day.

The inflation that has beset world capitalism in the recent past is not simply the result of capitalist *growth*, as Bell pretends; it is even more the product of capitalist *crisis*. The depression of the 1930s taught the rulers of this country that the monopoly-dominated capitalist economy, left to its own devices, inevitably led toward deep-going and prolonged crisis. Following the Second World War, they increasingly adopted the policies advanced by Keynes during the depression that would seek to provide "replacement markets" for inadequate normal ones through inflationary government deficit spending. "The avoidance of another Great Depression became the number one economic priority of the postwar world," monetary expert Irving Friedman wrote in 1973 (*Inflation*, p. 34).

"Government expenditure could supplement inadequate private investment; it would stimulate the economy in a way directly analogous to increased private investment. The consequences would be increased employment, increased income, increased demand—both for production and consumption goods. The economy could approach a new equilibrium, where employment, if not full, was greatly increased."

These policies were initiated during the war and postwar period primarily to build up the gigantic U.S. military machine. The inflationary war expenditures helped to stimulate the economy and defer another world depression, but that was not their essential purpose. They were and are primarily undertaken to build the weapons of the "arsenal of democracy"—that is, to defend and extend the empire of finance capital on a world scale. The countercyclical effect on the economy is a fringe benefit of this policy.

War-primed Inflation

One of the earliest documents in the Pentagon Papers brings out the continuity of the foreign policy of six postwar administrations, stretching from Democrat Harry Truman to Republican Gerald Ford, that have taken it upon themselves to police the global frontiers of capitalism. A telegram from General George C. Marshall, then secretary of state, to the U.S. Embassy in Paris, dated May 13, 1947, complains about the French failure to crush the Ho Chi Minh-led insurgents in Vietnam:

> We becoming increasingly concerned by slow progress toward settlement Indochina dispute. Key our position is awareness that in respect developments affecting position Western democratic powers in Southern Asia, we essentially in same boat as French, also British and Dutch. We cannot conceive setbacks to long-range interests France which would not also be setbacks our own. . . .
>
> In our view, southern Asia in critical phase its history with seven new nations in process achieving or struggling independence or autonomy. These nations include quarter inhabitants world and their future course, owing sheer weight populations, resources they command, and strategic location, will be momentous factor in world stability. . . . We consider best safeguard against these eventualities

a continued close association between newly-autonomous peoples and powers which have long been responsible for their welfare. [*United States-Vietnam Relations, 1945-1967*, Book 8, pp. 100-102]

Thus the author of the Marshall Plan and NATO, which supplied U.S. money, arms, and troops to capitalist Europe, also outlined a plan for inheriting the European colonies. The U.S. would support financially, and militarily if necessary, not only the French in Indochina, but the British in India, the Dutch in Indonesia, and above all the Kuomintang in China. "Pax Americana" was never an idle phrase. It meant money, guns, counterintelligence, and direct counterrevolutionary intervention by U.S. armies, in China, in Korea, in Lebanon, in Cuba, in the Congo, in Vietnam, in the Dominican Republic, in Cambodia, in Laos—wherever necessary and politically feasible. Meanwhile countless billions were spent year after year to build up the strategic arsenal of nuclear weapons, with its ability to annihilate the earth's population several times over.

These huge expenditures were only partially financed through taxation. To an increasing extent they were met through budget deficits, that is, by government borrowing. Including fiscal year 1976, there has only been one surplus budget year in the last sixteen. This was done because deficits were required to keep the economy growing—or, as has been the case for many years, stagnating rather than declining. It was also politically safer for Washington to raise part of its war expenditures indirectly through inflation than directly through taxes; and the inflation dampened and eventually rolled back the increases in real wages that had been won on picket lines. Inflation redistributed income to the strongest banks and largest corporations.

For those who still pretend that U.S. government deficits are attributable at least partially to social welfare expenditures, it must be pointed out that just the opposite is the case. Specific taxes are collected to finance these outlays (e.g., employment taxes, which pay Social Security, Medicare, Medicaid) and much more is collected in these taxes than is paid out. Total government debt that was held by such agencies in 1974 amounted to $141 billion. This surplus of funds, ostensibly earmarked for social welfare, has been invested in government bonds *in order to help defray massive military expenditures*.

It remains for us now to explain why government deficit spending on armaments is inflationary. To finance these deficits, the government must borrow from banks and other financial institutions. In order to meet the military expenses of the government without at the same time depleting the sources of money that the capitalists need to finance corporate business, the banking system must expand credit. This is especially true during economic upswings. It is *this expansion of credit by the banks,* in order to make funds available to corporations—much of which will be channeled into the government-guaranteed high-profit arena of war production—that *creates inflationary purchasing power in the economy.*

Government war spending is wholly unproductive. Unlike investment by industrial capitalists, the government's outlays do not transform the goods purchased into an expanded mass of commodities which are then put back on the market to be sold. Rather it simply takes goods off the market. The newly created purchasing power cannot find its equivalent on the market, and the monopolists *raise the prices on other goods* to absorb the "surplus purchasing power."

Some politicians and government officials seem to be indifferent to the inflationary impact of war spending. But the Pentagon Papers showed that the highest policy-makers were aware of the dangers of inflation from the outset of the cold war. Typical are the following paragraphs from National Security Council resolution 162/2, the "Basic National Security Policy" document of October 30, 1953, that enunciated Washington's global strategy:

> 21. Excessive government spending leads to inflationary deficits or to repressive taxation, or to both. Persistent inflation is a barrier to long-term growth because it undermines confidence in the currency, reduces savings, and makes restrictive economic controls necessary. . . .
> 27. The requirements for funds to maintain our national security must thus be considered in the light of these dangers to our economic system, including the danger to industrial productivity necessary to support military programs arising from excessive levels of total Government spending, taxing and borrowing. [*United States-Vietnam Relations,* Book 9, pp. 188, 189]

But these prophetic warnings were not observed over the next two decades. In August 1971, the "New Economic Policy" imposed "restrictive economic controls" in order to shore up the dollar, whose value had been eroded by years of war-primed inflation. The "NEP" showed that a turning point in postwar capitalist development had been reached.

The Meaning of the "NEP"

On December 27, 1971, the White House released to the corporations—but not to the American public—a white paper by then presidential assistant Peter G. Peterson explaining the "NEP." On the first page Peterson declared:

> The central fact of the past twenty-five years has been the conviction—ours as much as that of other countries—that the U.S. was dominant, both in size and competitiveness, in the international economy and that the practices, institutions and rules governing international trade and payments were structured to fit that fact. We as a nation and the world as a whole were too slow to realize that basic structural and competitive changes were occurring; as a result, international policies and practices were too slow in responding.

The weakened grasp of U.S. imperialism—not *Fortune*'s supposed demand-induced inflation—is the fundamental reason for the turn in U.S. and world economics. Although the precise date is not of critical importance, the turn had taken place before the Nixon-Connally offensive of 1971. Nixon's frontal attack on American workers in the form of a wage freeze, and his open declaration of international trade and financial warfare through an import surtax, dollar devaluation, and selective export controls, signaled that U.S. imperialism was in deep trouble. The crisis has significantly worsened in the succeeding period, even though 1972–73 saw a brief inflationary upturn in the world economy and there may well be further short-lived upturns. Overall, the direction for the foreseeable future is toward heightened attacks on the wages and living standards of workers both here and abroad.

There were two basic interrelated economic reasons why the turn in policy was inevitable:

1. The growth of postwar Europe and Japan provided the main outlets necessary for the expansionary drive of world capitalism. While the U.S economy reached high-level stagnation by the early fifties and frequently suffered recessions (the present is the sixth since World War II), these could be softened by exporting "overproduced" goods and capital abroad, primarily to Europe and Japan, but also to their former colonies whose markets had been wedged open by the U.S. victory in the war. In the process an explosive rise of productivity took place as new electronic and computer technologies were applied and millions of new workers were drawn into the labor forces of Europe, Japan, and North

America. But the European and Japanese "boom" ended. The markets it had provided were severely diminished.

2. The permanent inflation of the U.S. economy, which also helped to shore up domestic downturns, could be absorbed on a world scale and with minimal damage at home only so long as Europe and Japan were expanding, so long as they themselves did not have a great need for deficit financing. Simultaneous deficit spending on a world scale unleashed uncontrollable inflation.

The U.S. invasion of Southeast Asia hastened the culminating point of both these processes. On the one hand it qualitatively accelerated the rate of inflation in the United States, so that European and Japanese products became increasingly competitive both abroad and in the U.S. market itself, and the productivity gap was narrowed. On the other hand the war-primed inflation rapidly eroded the value of the dollar and destroyed the Bretton Woods international monetary system based on the gold-exchange standard. (For a Marxist history and analysis of this, see *Decline of the Dollar* by Ernest Mandel [New York: Monad Press, 1972].)

The new period was characterized by heightened competition in world trade. Its most prominent features so far have been the combined U.S.-Middle East imposition of high energy prices; the high prices of U.S. meat, grain, and soybean exports; a "floating" international exchange rate allowing continuous devaluation of the dollar as inflation continued to rage in the United States; increasingly sharp bouts of inflation internationally as well, as the major capitalist powers abroad also increasingly resorted to deficit spending. These developments have been accompanied by stepped-up attacks on workers everywhere, through direct wage freezes or controls ("austerity programs" in Europe), through the persistent decline of purchasing power caused by inflation, and through increasing bouts of joblessness as capitalist industry more and more failed to find profitable outlets for its goods and investments.

This veritable explosion of capitalist contradictions on a world scale once again demonstrated that the expansion of markets, even so large as those of Europe and Japan, cannot keep pace with the profit needs of monopoly.

The New U.S. Depression

Today the inflationary boomlet of 1972-73—perhaps one of the shortest in history—has given way to international recession and a depression in the United States. As in the late 1920s, overproduction occurred simultaneously in the two largest U.S. industries, auto and construction, which together account for more than 20 percent of the economy. Cutbacks in these sectors worked their way back through the industries that supply them with raw materials. More and more workers were laid off and, as purchasing power dropped, the recession deepened into depression.

By the spring of 1975 the manufacturing economy was operating at under 70 percent of its potential productive capacity. But it was still creating a Gross National Product of about $1,400 billion. If manufacturing were up to 100 percent of capacity, total production would be about $2,000 billion. The difference between what the economy is producing now and what it could produce if plants were fully operating is some $600 billion!

What a terrible waste this is of human and technical resources! It totals more than the Gross National Products of Latin America and Africa combined.

The criminality of wasted production at a time when millions are out of work, ill-fed, and unable to get a decent education or adequate health care is compounded by the fact that the depth and duration of the present downturn results from deliberate policies of the Ford administration. The most optimistic projections from the White House do not anticipate a substantial decline in unemployment in the foreseeable future. Full employment is not even a proclaimed goal.

While the rate of inflation has declined in the face of glutted markets, the huge government deficits anticipated for 1975–76 practically guarantee a resurgence of inflation more virulent than ever during the next upturn.

Under the conditions of sharpened international competition outlined by Peterson when he explained the "New Economic Policy," the American ruling class hopes to force the American populace into accepting not only the status quo but even a rollback of gains won and expectations generated in past struggles. The rulers want to dampen wage increases and diminish living standards; they would also like to see a reversal of the drive for equality by Black people and members of other oppressed minorities, of the women's rights movement, of demands for pollution control, and of the dissent against imperialist foreign policy.

On the economic front it is apparent that they have made some gains. *New York Times* reporter Damon Stetson noted April 7,

1975, that "continuing economic uncertainties and traumatic layoffs in many industries . . . have taken some of the steam out of union militants seeking large wage increases.

"'Fear has now replaced need as the gut issue,' one labor analyst said. . . .

"Among the approaches being talked about or tried in some cases are share-the-work arrangements, shorter work weeks [at less pay], payless furloughs, early retirements, and agreements to forego pay increases or even to take pay cuts."

The bourgeois ideologues of *Fortune* attempt to give a rationalization to the harsh economic realities that are a product of the depression and the administration's policies.

But they are shortsighted if they believe they will succeed in the larger scheme of stamping out the rising demands of the population. In fact, it can be predicted with assurance that the American working class, which has never suffered a serious defeat, will not accept this attempt to reverse its living standards and democratic rights without a fight. Already, despite the shackles imposed by bureaucratic misleaders, the labor movement is beginning to respond. Recent marches and rallies for jobs are steps in the direction of massive mobilizations of workers and their allies which—following the path of antiwar marchers before them—can raise sufficient protest to halt the capitalist offensive in its tracks.

As this confrontation develops, millions of workers will come to see that what is needed in the unions is a new class-struggle leadership with a strategy to meet their needs, a strategy that will lead to the elimination of capitalist exploitation and oppression once and for all.

*   *   *

An almost panicky atmosphere afflicted U.S. policy makers as they watched Saigon's armies melt away before the sweeping advance of the Vietnamese revolution in the spring of 1975. C. L. Sulzberger, the *New York Times*'s well-known foreign correspondent, turned in a column from Paris in which he declared: "No nation can pretend to be a superpower when its foreign policy suffers such blows as that of the United States in Southeast and Southwest Asia, when its economy reels, its currency staggers, and when its leadership, symbolized by a Chief Executive who chooses that moment to take time off for golf, faces its crises in paralyzed confusion.

"The lack of faith, morale, self-abnegation and willpower now being displayed on the ash-heap of a *pax Americana* cannot but appall our friends and comfort our enemies."

The gloom expressed by Sulzberger and the authors of the *Fortune* articles can only bring cheer and encouragement to oppressed peoples the world over who see the outposts of U.S. imperialism being weakened. The massive distrust of Americans toward the government in Washington and their deepgoing antiwar sentiment have combined with the advancing revolution in Southeast Asia and elsewhere to stay the arm of the U.S. imperialists as never before in this century. This crippling of its power enhances expectations of a different sort—that working people should have the direct decision-making power over their own future. And this runs diametrically counter to the monopolists' profit needs and global strategy.

Capitalism has demonstrated in the half century since 1929 that it *cannot* solve the pressing needs of humanity. In times of crisis it deals with the demands of the masses through depression, famine, and war. These lessons will be newly etched on the consciousness of workers, and that is what ideologues like Bell most fear. "It has become increasingly clear," he writes, "that the revolution of rising entitlements may become unmanageable. . . . If this process is not reversed, it will work to undermine the legitimacy of our society."

Precisely. But the right answer is not, as Bell urges, that workers should be persuaded to ask for less because capitalism can only give less. The workers should demand for themselves and for the oppressed of the world what is rightfully theirs—a liveable and peaceable existence. And if this is more than the decadent, crisis-torn system of world capitalism can give, it will have to give way to a new system.

APPENDIX

A Bill of Rights
for Working People

1976 campaign platform of Peter Camejo and Willie Mae Reid, presidential and vice-presidential candidates of the Socialist Workers Party

The United States is in a deepening crisis. We are in the midst of the worst depression since the 1930s. The quality of life for most people is going from bad to worse. And the present system offers us no hope for improvement.

There is no end to wars—one after another since the end of World War II. After Korea came Vietnam; now the Middle East is a powder keg. And Washington is looking for a way to help turn Portugal into the next Chile.

Huge stockpiles of hydrogen weapons are a constant reminder of the threat of nuclear war.

Pollution is destroying our environment—from the water we drink to the air we breathe.

Millions are unemployed, and layoffs throw more out of work every day. Breakdowns, shortages, and high prices—each week our real take-home pay is less. Suffering the most are those at the bottom of the ladder—Blacks, Chicanos, Puerto Ricans, women, and other doubly oppressed people.

Neither the Republican administration nor the Democratic Congress can offer a solution. They are only interested in shifting the responsibility and escaping the blame.

They try to pit white workers against Blacks in a struggle for jobs, housing, and education.

They blame all working people, claiming we eat too much and live too well. They say that inflation will slow down if we tighten our belts and stop demanding higher wages.

They blame people in other countries. They point to a "population explosion" in Asia, Africa, and Latin America as a burden on the U.S. economy—while the corporations they represent plunder the resources of these same countries.

They say the Arabs caused the energy crisis, as if skyrocketing profits of the U.S. oil monopolies weren't responsible.

The Democratic and Republican proposals are clear: don't struggle to defend your living standards; pay the costs of foreign wars; eat less and pay more; victimize foreign-born workers; use less electricity and gasoline; forget about health and safety, social services, and jobs.

This way of running the country can be stated in nine words: "What's good for big business is good for America."

The Rockefellers, DuPonts, Mellons, Morgans, and other super-rich families who rule America think they were born with rights and privileges that come before the welfare and security of the rest of us. For the sake of profits they think it is perfectly justifiable to lay off millions of workers, to destroy our environment, or to plunge the country into war.

They are a tiny minority trampling on the rights of the American people.

Defend the Rights of the Majority

Nearly 200 years ago, when our country won its war of independence against British tyranny, the workers and small farmers waged a fight to add ten amendments to the Constitution—the Bill of Rights. These were intended to help guarantee "life, liberty, and the pursuit of happiness."

Among these rights are:
- Freedom of speech, press, assembly, and religion
- Right to a jury trial by one's peers
- Right to bear arms
- Protection from unreasonable search and seizure, excessive bail or fines, and cruel or unusual punishment

A second revolution—the Civil War—resulted in additional amendments to the Constitution protecting the rights of the American people:
- Outlawing of slavery
- No deprivation of life, liberty, or property without due process of law
- Right of all male citizens age 21 or over to vote, regardless of race or color

More than fifty years ago women won the right to vote, and recently this was extended to all citizens over the age of 18.

These rights were won through struggle, and bitter battles have been required to preserve them against witch-hunters, racists, bigots, and antilabor forces. Especially significant was the recent victory of Blacks in the South, who fought for nearly two decades to restore voting rights forcibly denied them since the defeat of Reconstruction in the 1870s.

Yet all these rights have never been fully implemented, nor are they extended to everyone. In reality, millions of Americans are being pushed into second-class status by the powerful few who rule this country. Their whole strategy is to divide working people by trying to create a class of pariahs—oppressed minorities, women, foreign-born workers of color, the unemployed—those that relatively better-off white workers view as "them" rather than "us."

The only way to counter the rulers' attempts to undermine working class solidarity is for all working people to support the struggles of oppressed minorities and women for equal opportunities.

Preferential hiring and upgrading are necessary to help achieve equality on the job. Employers must not be allowed to use layoffs to reduce the proportion of minority and women workers.

To gain equality, Blacks and other oppressed minorities must have the right to live in the neighborhoods of their choice. They must have the right to decide where to send their children to school, and to use busing if necessary to transport them to better, predominantly white schools.

Minorities who don't speak English as their first language must be provided with education, civil service exams, ballots, and voting instructions in their own language to help achieve equality.

The struggle of women for the right to safe, legal abortions and to get the Equal Rights Amendment adopted and implemented should be supported to help achieve equality in all spheres of life.

Watergate revealed a tiny bit of the illegal spying, bugging, and harassment carried out by the government against unions, Black organizations, socialists, and other dissenters. Subsequent revelations have shown how the secret agencies coldly calculated to frame up people demanding their rights and then tried to sabotage their legal defense efforts—for example the American Indian Movement and the Attica defendants.

As the economic crisis deepens and big business tightens its squeeze on labor, the civil liberties of working people are threatened even more. Our rights to assembly, free speech, and individual privacy are being challenged.

Government interference infringes on the rights of unions to organize, bargain collectively, and strike. All laws that allow government interference in the unions or that bar public employees from striking should be repealed.

Democratic and human rights should be applied to prisoners, GIs, gays, foreign-born workers, and young people. Repressive legislation must be abolished, along with all cruel and unusual punishment including the death penalty.

A Bill of Rights for Working People

Not only is it necessary to fight back and reassert our rights, but we need to broaden these rights to protect working people against the threat of new wars, racist offensives, and attacks on our working conditions. We need a new bill of rights to meet the present needs of the majority, those who must work for a living. The Socialist Workers Party proposes the following:

1. Right to a job
2. Right to an adequate income, protected against inflation
3. Right to free education
4. Right to free medical care
5. Right to a secure retirement
6. Right of oppressed national minorities to control their own affairs
7. Right to know the truth about and decide the political policies that affect our lives
8. Right to know the truth about and decide economic and social policies

1. Right to a job

It is an elementary obligation of society to guarantee steady work for everyone. This can be done by the following measures:

An emergency public works program should be launched to provide jobs through construction of housing, mass transportation, hospitals, schools, child care facilities, parks, and other social necessities. Priority should be given to projects in the workers' neighborhoods, where they are most needed—especially in Black, Chicano, and Puerto Rican communities.

The huge sums necessary to pay for this program should come from eliminating the mammoth war budget and from a 100 percent tax on war profits. A moratorium should be declared on using our taxes to pay billions of dollars to bankers for interest on the public debt.

Working hours should be reduced with no reduction in take-home pay in order to spread the available work and achieve full employment.

Unemployment compensation should be paid by the government at full union wages for as long as a person is unemployed.

In order to assure economic independence for women, government-financed free child care centers should be established. Maternity leaves with full pay should be provided. Women must also have the right to decide whether or not to give birth to children. This includes the right to abortion and contraception on demand as well as protection from forced sterilization.

And fellow workers who are not U.S. citizens, including those without immigration documents, are entitled to jobs and equal pay without fear of racist harassment or deportation.

2. Right to an adequate income protected against inflation

A guaranteed living wage is a basic human right. As a protection against inflation, wages must be free to rise. There must be no government wage controls.

To offset price gouging on food, rent, gas, electricity, and other basic necessities, wages must be protected with cost-of-living escalator clauses in union contracts, so that wages increase—promptly and fully—with each rise in living costs.

Escalator provisions should be pegged to the real rate of inflation as determined by committees set up by unions and consumer groups—not the Labor Department's Consumer Price Index which is based on a "market basket" that deliberately underestimates price increases.

All pensions, Social Security benefits, unemployment and disability compensation, welfare and veterans' benefits should be raised to union wage scales and protected with cost-of-living escalator provisions.

Small working farmers, who are gouged by banks on one hand and squeezed by the food trusts on the other, should be allowed to make a decent living. They have a right to low-interest, long-term government loans.

3. Right to free education
4. Right to free medical care
5. Right to a secure retirement

Education, health, and security should not be privileges of the rich. These are rights that should be guaranteed to everyone. They are the responsibility of society.

Tuition, books, and living expenses should be furnished to all who want to attend colleges and trade schools.

Everyone, from birth to old age, should be guaranteed free medical and dental care through a full program of socialized medicine.

All retired and disabled persons should receive government-financed benefits at full union wages.

Government-financed programs should be instituted not only to provide care for people who are ill, but for medical research and public education about health.

Adult education and cultural programs should be expanded to permit working people to develop themselves to the fullest extent possible.

6. Right of oppressed national minorities to control their own affairs

Blacks, Chicanos, Puerto Ricans, and other oppressed peoples have a right to control the schools, hospitals, child care centers, parks, and other institutions in their communities. They have a right to determine how federal and state funds will be used in their communities.

To end police brutality and lower the crime rate, the police should be removed from the ghettos and barrios. They should be replaced with a security force democratically selected and supervised by the people who live in these communities.

7. Right to know the truth about and decide political policies that affect our lives

Republican and Democratic administrations claim that their foreign policy decisions advance peace and democracy throughout the world. The Pentagon Papers, the CIA's intervention in Chile, and Nixon's secret promise to the Thieu regime to send U.S. troops and B-52s back into Vietnam show that this is not true. We have a right to know the full truth. Let us see what the rulers really have in mind when they make decisions that affect our lives:

Publish all secret treaties and agreements Washington has made with other countries!

Open all police, CIA, FBI, and IRS files!

No secret diplomacy behind the backs of the American people!

Let the public know the truth about U.S. support for dictatorships all over the world, from South Africa to South Korea.

Take the war-making power away from the White House and Congress. Let the people vote in a referendum before the country is dragged into any more wars. Let us have the right to say no to policies that can lead to nuclear holocaust and the end of humanity.

We have the right to say no to government stockpiling and testing of weapons that threaten our health and safety and endanger the ecology. We have a right to veto the stationing of U.S. forces throughout the world and support of puppet military dictators.

8. Right to know the truth about and decide economic and social policies

When the corporations claim they can't grant wage increases, and when they lay off workers, make them *open their books.*

Make the oil, food, and auto monopolies show their records to elected workers' committees so we can see their real profits, production statistics, technological possibilities, and secret dealings. Then we can see who is rigging prices, deliberately creating shortages, and hoarding reserves.

When employers close down plants, those plants should be *nationalized* and put under the control of these workers' committees. With access to all financial and technical information kept secret by the bosses, the workers' committees will be able to make the necessary decisions on retooling and reopening the plants to produce for the needs of society.

These workers' committees can expose the hundreds of business secrets that tie industry and agribusiness to the big banks, the transportation and retailing monopolies, government agencies, Democratic and Republican politicians, and judges.

Workers have the right to control their working conditions through their own democratically elected committees. They have the right to regulate the pace of work in the safest and least dehumanizing way.

Workers—for example, the miners—have a right to elect their own safety inspectors. Production must be shut down on the demand of the workers and at the expense of the boss whenever the safety of personnel is involved.

Workers have a right to halt industrial processes that contaminate the air and water and endanger the environment.

They have a right to veto arbitrary and discriminatory layoffs.

Workers also have a right to insist that things they produce will be safe and durable and that production will be for social needs rather than private profits.

When monopolies like the utilities, the postal service, the railroads, and the airlines cry bankruptcy, charge exorbitant rates, or refuse services to those who can't pay their rates, they should be nationalized and operated under the control of workers' committees.

In order to make sound decisions, these committees will have to cooperate with similar committees throughout their industry on a national scale and in other industries in their region, as well as with committees of consumers, housewives, and other affected groups.

To acquire the needed information and resources for economic planning, the entire banking system—in reality the accounting and credit system of the capitalist class—will have to be taken over, opened up to the workers' committees, and placed under their control.

Only in that way can the entire economy be democratically planned and organized so as to prevent the recurring breakdowns and chaos that result from the anarchy of production for private profit.

If the majority had known the truth about the oil industry and had the right to make the decisions about the country's energy needs, the energy crisis would have been prevented. The oil trusts deliberately cut back their refining capacity in order to create a shortage and drive up prices and profits. A national plan worked out and overseen by the workers themselves would not have allowed this to happen.

Such a national economic plan would divert the colossal sums now spent for military purposes to social needs. It would end the threat of worldwide famine and war.

However, this will only be possible if the government itself passes completely into the hands of the majority—the masses of working people.

For a Workers' Government

When the American colonists could no longer tolerate British rule and drew up their Declaration of Independence, they stated that "whenever any form of government becomes destructive of these ends [life, liberty, and the pursuit of happiness], it is the right of the people to alter or to abolish it, and to institute new government, laying its foundation on such principles, and organizing its powers in such form, as to them shall seem most likely to effect their safety and happiness."

Today we are ruled by a new tyranny. Industrial and financial barons govern us by the rule of profits, denying the basic democratic and social rights we need for life, liberty, and the pursuit of happiness. This government of the few must be abolished and replaced by a workers' government that will represent the majority.

A workers' government will guarantee democracy and implement a new bill of rights for working people.

It will immediately recognize the right of Blacks and Chicanos to self-determination. It will immediately grant independence to Puerto Rico.

It will end all discrimination against foreign-born workers and extend them equal rights with all other workers.

It will adopt a policy of peace and friendship with peoples throughout the world and offer massive economic and technical assistance and food to other countries—with no strings attached. It will stop U.S. interference in the internal affairs of other countries and dismantle all U.S. military bases abroad. It will stop shedding the blood of America's youth in foreign adventures.

Instead of supporting oppressors and dictators, it will aid the struggles of the oppressed—Palestinians driven from their homeland by Israel; South African Blacks ruled by a white minority; South Koreans dominated by U.S.-backed generals, bankers, and landlords; Chileans repressed by the bloody military junta.

A workers' government in the United States would be a tremendous inspiration to people all over the world. With a knowledge that the mighty USA was not their enemy, oppressed people everywhere would rise up against their oppressors. The entire world would be changed for the better.

The working people of the Soviet Union would throw out their hated rulers and revive the democratic and humanitarian goals of the Russian Revolution. The hand of friendship would be extended between the Soviet and American peoples, and the threat of nuclear war would be eliminated. Socialist democracy would open up a new epoch for humanity.

How Can These Goals Be Achieved?

The majority can win its rights only by its own independent

action. *Rallies* de_ nding jobs for all; *strikes* for higher wages and cost-of-living clauses; *demonstrations* against new war threats, against cu: ,acks in education and social services, and for the rights of women; a *boycott* of scab lettuce, grapes, and wine; *marches* against racist attacks on busing and school desegregation—these are examples of struggles now being waged.

But it doesn't make sense to strike, rally, demonstrate, boycott, or march against the deterioration of our rights and living standards on one day, and then vote for the two parties responsible for it on the next.

The colonists fighting British rule and the abolitionists fighting against slavery learned that they could have no faith in the goodwill of colonial governors or the slave-owners' parties.

They formed their own organizations, including committees of correspondence, continental congresses, and Black conventions.

Likewise today, working people cannot rely on the Democratic and Republican parties, which are financed and controlled by big business to defend its profits. We must break from them.

The Socialist Workers Party believes that the only way to effectively organize the power of American working people on the scale necessary to abolish the present government of big business, and initiate a workers' government, is through a mass socialist party. This will not be anything like the Democratic and Republican parties; it will be a fighting party that will help lead the struggles of working people and all the oppressed. This is what the Socialist Workers Party is campaigning for and what it intends to become.

The first big step toward a working class break from the two parties of big business would be the formation of an independent *labor party* based on the power of the unions. Workers running as independent labor candidates on a local scale can help set an example and point the way to a nationwide party of labor. Such a party would organize union power into a new social movement to fight for the rights of *all* the oppressed. It would lead the way toward a mass socialist movement that can start building a new social system.

The Socialist Workers Party is campaigning for a new society— a socialist society—where industry and science will be put at the service of the vast majority; where wars, racism, sexual oppression, and all other forms of human degradation and exploitation will no longer exist. We believe that this is a realistic goal, and a necessary one if humanity is to survive.

Join us in this struggle.

The Capitalist
World Economic Crisis

A resolution adopted by the International Executive Committee of the Fourth International, January 1975

Despite the years of propaganda that it would never again occur, the capitalist world has plunged into its first generalized recession since the 1930s. While it would be hazardous to forecast that world unemployment levels will rise as high as in the Great Depression, the threat has not been eliminated. A heightened offensive of capital against labor's living standards is under way everywhere. No long-term respite from inflation is possible in any of the major powers.

1. The current recession of the international capitalist economy was predicted by revolutionary socialists long in advance. Between 1948 and 1973 capitalist world production increased three and a half times at an average rate of 5 percent a year. There was no growth in 1974. By the last quarter of 1974, industrial output of all major imperialist countries was declining. The United States is in its deepest postwar economic downturn, with the Gross National Product (GNP) down 2.2 percent from 1973. It is falling fast. The GNP fell 3 percent in Japan, after twenty-five years of expansion.

Only some of the minor capitalist countries have as yet escaped the immediate effects of the decline (Sweden, Switzerland, Norway, Austria), either because of exceptional circumstances (the discovery of North Sea oil for Norway) or because of their particular relationship to the world market.

The physical volume of world trade has not yet declined, although the rate of growth has dropped sharply. The major powers are seeking to step up foreign sales, if possible, to counteract the recession at home. Whether the volume of world trade will decline depends on the length of the downturn in the major countries (above all the United States, West Germany, and

Japan) and on the extent of protectionist measures undertaken by the competing powers.

While the actual downturn in industrial output is still small (except in the United States) the rise in unemployment is pronounced. Indeed, official figures in the imperialist countries for the winter of 1974-75 may show that unemployment has risen above 15 million. This will certainly prove to be the case if in addition to those listed as unemployed account is taken of those who work only part-time because full-time jobs are not available to them. Unemployment is probably around 8 to 10 million in the United States; 1.5 million in Italy; 1 million each in West Germany, France, and Britain; 1 million in the minor imperialist countries of Western Europe (Benelux countries, Spain, Denmark, etc.); 1 million in Japan; and 1 million in Canada, Australia, and New Zealand taken together.

The reasons for this disproportionate increase in unemployment are twofold:

(a) The present worldwide economic crisis follows a long period of rapid technological progress (automation) in which productivity rose steeply, especially in Western Europe and Japan (this occurred earlier in the United States). The technological advance was accompanied as always by a slow erosion of the rate of profit, which capital attempted to offset through speedups, "rationalization," and other methods of reducing labor costs. But when the rate of increase of productivity is high, only a substantial increase in output can avoid massive unemployment. If there is an actual decline or even mere stagnation in output, unemployment will soar.

(b) In the imperialist countries since World War II, there has been a dramatic increase in the number of women seeking employment. There are two main reasons for this development. One is that average wages for males (whether industrial or "white collar") are no longer adequate to satisfy the basic needs of a working-class family. The other is that women are displaying greater economic and social independence, a reflection internationally of the women's liberation movement.

This growing trend, together with that of mounting seasonal appearances of students on the labor market, has increased the potential supply of labor power in the job market independently of the cyclical fluctuations of the economy. Among the workers seeking employment in the imperialist countries are growing layers that are sexually, racially, and nationally oppressed (in the United States, Blacks, Chicanos, and members of other oppressed nationalities; in Western Europe, immigrant workers), a fact that has facilitated the formation of a large actual or potential industrial reserve army of labor, even during periods of high employment levels.

2. The current international capitalist recession constitutes a turning point in postwar developments of immense significance.

(a) *It is the first generalized recession since the thirties.* There have been many recessions since World War II. Indeed, today as in the past, capital cannot avoid cyclical fluctuations of its economy. But the staggered character of these recessions (for example, the absence of a recession in West Germany, Japan, Italy, and France during the severe 1957-58 U.S. downturn) limited their breadth and depth. A country with shrinking internal markets could export surplus goods and capital.

But with all the major imperialist countries caught simultaneously, the export markets are pinched off. The possibility of finding a solution by increasing exports to the bureaucratized workers' states and the oil-exporting countries of the Middle East is likewise excluded. These potential markets are minimal compared to what is required to absorb the mounting surplus of capital and commodities.

Because it occurs simultaneously in many countries, the recession can build up as a whole with extraordinary force, the recession in each country aggravating the recessions in the others, and all of them combining to make the crisis much graver than any recession since the thirties. The danger is particularly great if the recession in the United States lasts through 1975. The United States produces almost as much as all the other twenty-three member nations of the Organization of Economic Cooperation and Development (OECD), a group comprising all the major capitalist countries. Because of its massiveness, the U.S. economy tends to draw the others into its orbit.

(b) *The present international recession clearly confirms previous observations that the long postwar capitalist boom had come to an end.*

The long period of accelerated economic growth following World War II included cyclical downturns; but they were shorter and less intense than those of the twenties and thirties; and the economic and social consequences for the masses were much less dramatic. In addition to the impulse given to world capitalism by the rebuilding of Europe and Japan following the devastation of World War II, the massive use of "anticrisis" measures by the imperialist governments tended to soften economic downturns, although the end result was merely to postpone the reckoning and entrench permanent inflation.

Particularly important has been armaments spending in the United States. Year after year Washington has poured colossal sums into the national and world economy to arm and finance military forces in the United States and abroad, and to pay the increasingly large interest on accumulated military debts. The budget deficits to carry out these operations have become staggering (figures ranging from $52 billion to $70 billion have been mentioned for the U.S. budgetary deficit in the fiscal year beginning July 1975).

The "pump-priming" nostrum of government deficit spending was not limited to the United States. By 1973 all the major capitalist powers were throwing huge amounts into deficit spending. The rapid expansion of credit on a world scale drove up prices everywhere.

Moreover, each successive recession required bigger doses of inflationary deficit spending to block a worse slump. This became a vicious circle.

Increasing inflation of the dollar led to a series of crises and ultimately to the collapse in 1971 of the international monetary system set up at Bretton Woods in 1944, marking the end of the long postwar boom.

The short inflationary boom of 1971–73 was merely a passing phase in the opening of a new long-term period of increasingly aggravated contradictions of world capitalism (including much slower growth) that began in 1967–68 and that became still more clearly manifested in the present world recession.

3. *The present recession is fundamentally a classical crisis of overproduction caused by the inner contradictions of the capitalist mode of production.* It is not an accident, allegedly caused by the "oil sheiks," any more than the 1929 depression was caused by "speculation" in stocks, or previous serious economic crises were caused by "overextending" railway construction or overseas trade.

To be sure, each crisis of overproduction appears as a combination of general phenomena arising from the very nature of capitalist production, and particular phenomena brought to the fore at a given phase of its worldwide expansion and ups and downs. But the very fact that these "accidents" occur with a regular periodicity, that they can be foreseen and predicted, and that they have a whole series of common features, shows that they are bound up structurally with the capitalist system itself.

Neither the precapitalist nor the postcapitalist economies undergo these cyclical fluctuations of employment, industrial output, and national income.

Likewise, the ultimate causes of the present worldwide recession are the inner contradictions of the capitalist mode of production long ago laid bare by Marx. After a period of economic growth, the tendency of the rate of profit to decline necessarily becomes more prominent. This holds with all the greater force the longer the period of growth and the faster its rate. The organic composition of capital increases as automation and semiautomation reinforce the preponderance of machinery and other forms of stored-up "dead labor" in production. The classical avenues for offsetting the effects of the rising organic composition of capital are more and more obstructed.

High employment levels and the growing social and organizational strength of the working class make it increasingly difficult for capital to significantly raise the rate of exploitation (the rate of surplus value).

The very attempts of capital to cheapen raw materials create divergent trends in prices and profits in primary products on the one hand and manufactured goods on the other. This leads to a growing disproportion in capital investments and current production in both sectors. Sooner or later this results in a relative scarcity of raw materials and to a radical increase in their prices as compared to those of manufactured goods.

The decline in the rate of profit combined with an intensification of competition, in turn, creates the need for borrowing a larger and larger part of the capital needed for additional investments. This is the source of the increasingly severe "liquidity crises" of private companies both nationally and internationally.

But even the biggest corporations can meet insurmountable difficulties in raising the funds required for profitable investment. At a given point all these forces pressing down on the rate of profit must lead to a growing number of capitalist firms being threatened by bankruptcy or actually becoming bankrupt, to an overall decrease in the volume of investment (of capital accumulation), to a massive curtailment of production, to massive layoffs, which by their cumulative effects create a generalized downturn in economic activity.

On the other hand, there is an inherent trend in capitalist production to extend productive capacity beyond the limited purchasing power of the masses, which is determined in the last analysis by the antagonistic class relations within bourgeois society. Each capitalist boom creates a tendency toward excess capacity and overproduction and the consequent stockpiling of unsellable commodities in key sectors of the economy. As this excess capacity and overproduction increases, current output and employment are correspondingly curtailed, and the crisis is worsened accordingly.

In the present recession, overproduction began in the automobile industry and the building trades. It spread rapidly to electrical appliances, petrochemicals (plastics and synthetic fibers), textiles and clothing, the tourist trade, and aviation industries. It has now reached even the steel industry, which a few months ago was still in the midst of one of its biggest booms, resulting from the drastic concentration and curtailment of investment in that industry in the late 1960s and relative scarcity of steel that resulted in the beginning of the 1970s.

4. While stressing the general structural causes of the present world recession, the analysis should pinpoint the special aspects that differentiate it from previous overproduction crises, especially the big slumps of 1929-33 and of 1937-38:

(a) The main distinguishing feature is *world inflation*. A sharp increase in prices coincided with the opening of the recession. *The world capitalist economy passed from an inflationary boom through "stagflation" toward "slumpflation."* In the past, a sharply downward movement, if not an actual collapse of prices, occurred in depressions. Inflation coincided with crises only in exceptional circumstances—lost wars, civil wars, complete disruption of the economy and output; and then only for a short time.

Today world inflation is continuing (and in certain countries like the United States, Britain, Italy, France, even increasing!) in spite of a downturn in production and employment. This disrupts the "normal" function of an overproduction crisis. It is supposed to restabilize the economy by eliminating the more backward firms, clearing out inventories, and increasing the rate of exploitation, thereby paving the way for renewed investment.

But the inflationary expansion of credit prolongs inventory buildup, concealing the actual weaknesses of firms. For a time, the increase in nominal wages cloaks the erosion of real wages. Artificial purchasing power is created—artificial for firms that ultimately will not be able to remain competitive; artificial for workers who simply cannot repay debts once the lowering of real wages and outright unemployment has reached a certain point.

Thus the expansion of credit can go too far. It can prepare the way for unexpected bankruptcies and the closing of banks; in other words, precisely the kind of credit collapse nationally and internationally that characterized the depression of the 1930s. The imperialists themselves do not rule out this danger.

(b) Another distinguishing factor of the world recession is the combination of recession in most sectors of output, including key raw materials, *with an acute shortage in two central sectors of the world capitalist economy: energy (especially oil) and food (especially grain and sugar).*

This combination is not a result of "natural catastrophes," nor does it express the "limits of growth" of the productive forces. It is a result of disproportions created by monopoly competition.

Relatively low prices of raw materials lead to an outflow of capital from this sector into other sectors. Shortages are a means of increasing profits and attracting new capital. This objective process, in turn, can be accelerated by deliberate decisions of the monopolists.

The international petroleum cartel (the seven "oil majors") curtailed refinery capacity and oil production as part of a policy of driving up world energy prices and profits. In the interest of higher prices and profits, U.S., Canadian, and Australian "agribusiness" curtailed food production. This is the root cause of the current famines in the African Sahel countries and the Indian subcontinent.

These specific features of the world recession have to be taken into account to evaluate its economic, social, and political effects on various countries, parts of the world, and social classes. But they in no way change the estimate of the world recession as a deep crisis of the capitalist system as a whole.

5. Theoretically and technically, a transformation of the present world recession into a depression of the 1929-32 type is not excluded. It could occur if the governments of the imperialist countries fail (for objective or subjective reasons) to follow economic policies aimed at mitigating the downturn. Such a depression could occur if aggregate demand in the key imperialist countries were cut by strong reductions of government outlays and by major curtailment of credit coinciding with big increases in unemployment and sharp declines in wages and profits.

Such occurrence would imply:

Either (a) that for some objective reason outside of the control of the capitalist governments (for example, a collapse of confidence in paper money, including the dollar, the deutsche mark, etc., leading to a return to gold as the only final means of payment for international operations) a strong deflationary trend appears in money and credit in all the major imperialist countries, a trend that coincides with overproduction. This is what happened in 1929-32, ultimately provoking international bank failures.

Or (b) that a trend appears among the capitalist governments to press for general deflation of the volume of money and credit in order to radically "cure" inflation even if it means 30 to 40 million unemployed on a world scale.

While the second course is technically possible, it is highly unlikely. Even an unemployment level of a half or a third the scale of the 1930s is frightening enough to governments to induce them to revive inflationary policies (as is already the case in Washington and Bonn).

The world recession occurs at a time in the class struggle when the level of working-class organization and the capacity for resistance are immensely stronger than in 1929 or 1937. It occurs at a time when the world relationship of forces between imperialism and its various antagonists is much more unfavorable to world capital than before World War II. Under these circumstances a catastrophic economic depression of the 1929-32 type would engender an explosive social and political crisis not only in Western Europe but also in Japan and North America.

If unemployment levels reached 15 million in the United States, 5 million in West Germany, 5 million in Japan, 3 million unemployed in Britain, France, and Italy, short-term palliatives would not avert the intense anger and explosive reaction of the working class. The example of large-scale noncapitalist planned economies that are able to avoid unemployment and inflation despite their bureaucratic deformations would help inspire the Western working class to break out of the private profit system, giving the thrust toward socialism immense force as the masses noted the most effective tactical expedients used in other lands. *A repetition of a 1929-32 type of depression would, under the present international and national sociopolitical relationship of forces, clearly initiate the gravest crisis of the capitalist system since its inception.*

To avoid such a catastrophe for themselves, the imperialist governments will likely refrain from the ruthless kind of deflation of money and credit volume that made the 1929-32 depression unavoidable. The strongest ones still have sufficient reserves to follow such a course. They have no alternative but to continue, in their characteristically pragmatic and sometimes even panicky way, to oscillate between anti-inflationary and antirecessionary measures in such a way as not to trigger "too much" unemployment or "too high" prices. They can stop neither!

Nevertheless the question can legitimately be asked: Is it not possible that even the key imperialist governments will lose control over the situation? It seems obvious that inflation cannot continue indefinitely without exhausting its antirecessionary effects and even transforming itself from a motor into a brake on capitalist economic growth. The collapse of the speculative boom in 1973 and early 1974; the bankruptcies of several important banks; the huge losses met by speculators in currencies, in raw materials, and in land; the collapse of stock prices in the main stock exchanges throughout the capitalist world—all these were ominous signs of a potential worldwide panic. The tremendous extension of the Eurodollar market (additionally fueled by "petrodollars"), the threat of a massive balance-of-payments deficit in nearly all the imperialist countries (with the exception of West Germany) as a result of the steep increase in their oil import bill, threatened to provoke a sudden collapse of confidence and a resulting worldwide run on the banking system.

Following the collapse of the Franklin National Bank in the United States, I. D. Herstatt of West Germany, and the crisis of the "fringe banks" in Britain, major central banks promised to support rescue operations in behalf of the depositors and, to a certain extent, they will attempt to do this in other cases so as to head off a crash. But these cases also illustrated the limits of such operations. When West Germany refused at first to back Herstatt deposits, the United States retaliated by threatening to freeze West German assets and brought the international monetary system grinding to a halt until the secret deals were arranged. The European-American Bank which was formed to take over Franklin National has warned that it will take almost none of Franklin's foreign accounts.

In the same category, the United States has recently warned all U.S. banks to review their medium- and long-term loans to Italian industry and to the Italian government itself. The anti-Arab and anti-Iranian propaganda mounted around "petrodollars" by the imperialist banking circles is aimed at helping to force the oil-exporting nations into international credit-rescue operations that the imperialists themselves are unwilling to undertake.

All of these examples illustrate the fact that the self-interest of national capitalism places severe limits on the degree to which central bankers can alleviate the international crisis.

The deeper and more lasting the inflation, the greater the danger becomes that speculation, debts, and liquidity crises of the banking system will mount to such proportions as to touch off a panicky run on the banks, resulting in a collapse of the banking system and a consequent catastrophic crisis, if not now, then in a future recession. That is why the world bourgeoisie is so worried about inflation. That is why it is trying to alter the class relationship of forces sufficiently to make feasible the eventual use of radical deflationary measures.

6. What makes the present situation so grave for world capitalism, however, is not so much the fact that the economic crisis is the worst yet experienced in the postwar period—it is still much milder than those that occurred between the two world wars—*but that it is combined with an exceptionally high level of organization, striking power, and militancy of the working class.* The situation in the working class is a resultant of two decades of relatively high economic growth, of a relatively high level of employment, of extensive (Japan, Italy, France, Spain, Canada, Australia) and intensive (United States, West Germany, Britain) industrialization, and a general increase in the level of skills and education (even if spread very unevenly and accompanied by massive downgrading, marginalization, and scrapping of workers). Additional factors have strengthened the working class subjectively. These include the worldwide radicalization of youth and women; the advances of the world revolution in the semicolonial countries from China to Cuba; the appearance of a new generation of workers who did not experience the two and a half decades of defeats following the October 1917 victory; the crisis of Stalinism; and a generalized increase in opposition to imperialist war.

This means that the *present social crisis of the world capitalist system,* which began with the May 1968 events in France, *will be seriously and significantly deepened by the present recession,* and that the central role of the industrial working class will become increasingly accentuated.

But it also means that the general trend points to increasing tensions and explosive conflicts between capital and labor, of more and more acute political crises in key imperialist countries. Attempts of the capitalists to "buy off" workers will decline relatively while attempts to inflict serious defeats upon the working class will increase, the objective being to "solve" the crisis at the expense of workers by reducing real wages, thereby enabling the rate of profit to rise again. Such an onslaught on the living standard and level of employment of the working class entails serious restrictions on the democratic rights of the working class (statutory wage controls, government arbitration of labor disputes, onerous limitations on the right to strike, antiunion legislation, etc.).

Experience has shown, however, that as long as capital is unable to succeed in significantly changing the existing relationship of forces between the classes, the attempts to apply such policies generally fail.

This does not exclude short-term attempts to head off revolutionary victories through reforms and concessions. But, as in the 1930s, these will amount to no more than stopgap measures. The aggravation of the world economic situation rules out any significant period of decreasing tension between the classes. It brings class confrontations closer to a showdown. The broad perspective is either the revolutionary overthrow of capitalism, or grave defeats of the working class that will enable capitalism to apply *its* solution—fascism even more brutal than that of the 1930s.

7. In the present world recession, the proletariat stands in a much stronger position than was the case in the 1929-32 depression. Among other things, unemployment is not of such scope and duration as in the Great Depression and has had less of a debilitating effect.

Massive unemployment for a long period is generally highly demoralizing. The most favorable moments for workers' actions are either when unemployment starts (that is why the international bourgeoisie is so afraid that sudden massive unemployment could provoke an immediate reaction in the proletariat) or when it begins to decline after an economic revival has started. But during a period of mass unemployment those who do hold jobs are exceptionally fearful of losing them, the employed and unemployed become pitted against each other, as do the partially and fully employed, and those who have a relatively high level of job security and those who lack it. All these factors tend to limit the number and duration of strikes.

Of course, certain modifications have to be made in this general analysis. In particular, it is necessary to take into account the "built-in stabilizers" such as unemployment insurance, social security, the dole, low-cost health services, etc., that were introduced during or after the 1929-32 crisis.

However, unemployment on a limited scale, such as still exists in the major imperialist countries, has none of these debilitating effects, especially in view of its combination with inflation and with the growing level of organization and militancy of the working class. Therefore it can be safely predicted that the *immediate effect of the world recession will be to fortify the upsurge of workers' struggles* (with the short-term exception of West Germany, for specific reasons linked with the whole postwar cycle of class struggles and class consciousness in that country).

In Western Europe, the recession will impel a sharpening of class struggles and class tensions especially in those countries where the working-class upsurge has reached the highest level: France, Italy, Britain, Spain, Portugal, but also in minor capitalist countries like Denmark. It will tend to shift the axis more and more away from partial struggles to generalized struggles, and give increasing impulse to the search for overall political solutions to the deep-going social crisis of capitalism.

The upswing of working-class radicalization and militancy in the United States and Japan (as well as Australia, New Zealand, and Canada) will tend to be accelerated by the generalized recession, the proletariat in these countries thereby beginning to fall more into the pattern seen in Western Europe since 1968. It is still too early, however, to predict the forms and rates of this process. The more the Japanese, American, and Canadian working classes move into action in the coming years, adding their weight to the present upsurge of struggle in Western Europe, the greater will be the impact on an international scale and the more difficult it will be for world capitalism to "solve" its present crisis at the expense of this or that sector of the world working class.

8. The intensification of interimperialist rivalries was one of the causes that precipitated the worldwide recession in 1974. Far from responding as a whole in ways that would tend to ward off a world recession and possible financial collapse, the competing capitalist nations have mainly pursued narrow policies of self-interest. Moreover, no imperialist power or group of imperialist powers, including the most powerful of all—the United States itself—is able to impose its own competitive interests on all sectors of the world bourgeoisie as operative guidelines.

Interimperialist rivalries have aggravated the contradictions underlying the recession. From the standpoint of the overall interests of international capitalism, the use of anti-inflationary (mildly deflationary) policies simultaneously in all the major imperialist countries obviously does not make sense. But from the standpoint of each capitalist class taken separately, it makes sense to "fight inflation" and to try to save its currency and banking system from collapse.

Here there are three concerns: to keep foreign goods out of the domestic market by keeping the prices of domestic goods lower; to penetrate foreign markets to a greater degree because prices of foreign goods are higher; and to stabilize the domestic currency by maintaining a less rapid rate of inflation. Thus, in the era of simultaneous world inflation, the fight to keep one's "own" rate of inflation lower than the rates of competitors becomes a central preoccupation of the competing bourgeoisies. Each major power would like to shift part of the burden of inflation and the recession onto its competitors.

West Germany, for example, maintained deflationary policies right up to December 1974, when the specter of world collapse had already been haunting stock exchanges for most of the year. It held to this course despite increasing pressure from its competitors for "reflation" of the deutsche mark, since West Germany is the only major imperialist country that is not suffering from a balance of payments deficit as a result of the increase in oil prices.

A strong reflation of the West German economy would mean that German exports (which have now overtaken those of the United States) would suffer seriously, while the West German internal market would yield a larger share to imports from its British, French, Italian, Japanese, and U.S. competitors.

But when unemployment reached 3.5 percent in West Germany and threatened to go to 4 percent, Bonn dropped its anti-inflationary program. Pump-priming government expenditures were announced, the central bank's discount rate was lowered, and West German capitalism will now try another round in gambling against the rates of inflation elsewhere.

The 1973-74 oil crisis marked a shift in the inter-imperialist relationship of forces in favor of U.S. imperialism, since the United States is less dependent on oil imports than the other major imperialist powers and the capitalists in Western Europe had for years paid less for oil (and energy) than those in the U.S.

Meanwhile, however, the stepped-up export drive, especially of West Germany and Japan, has partially annulled the results gained by Wall Street through the successive devaluations of the dollar and the oil crisis. Yet France, and especially Britain and

Italy, have been less successful with their export drives and as a result have been harder hit by the worldwide rise in oil prices, both Britain and Italy undergoing very severe economic and financial difficulties.

Furthermore, the failure to seriously advance their economic integration during the present recession, which threatens to bring down the Common Market, prevents the West German and West European capitalists from offering a plausible alternative leadership to the world capitalist system.

Under these conditions, the crisis of leadership of international capitalism as a whole is compounded by the crisis of leadership of the bourgeoisies in each of the major imperialist nations. This will not change in the near future, all the more so as the intensification of the class struggle adds to the crisis in each country. The first bourgeoisie to succeed in imposing a major social and political defeat on "its" working class would, as in the 1930s, gain a significant margin for maneuver, enabling it to engage in dangerous attempts at changing the world relationship of forces in its favor. But again, this is unlikely to occur in the near future.

The outcome will be endless consultations, horsetrading, and shady deals, a rigamarole that will become all the more agonizing as the recession drags on.

9. In the semicolonial countries, the effect of the world recession varies according to the relation of their economies to oil, grain, and sugar imports and exports. Those that are large exporters of these vital raw materials, and that have only a small deficit (or no deficit) of these high-priced commodities, have, so far, not suffered from the present recession. (A collapse of sugar prices and a sharp decline of oil prices cannot be excluded if the recession is long lasting, although even in this case oil prices will not drop to pre–October 1973 levels.)

The ruling classes of the major oil-exporting countries have benefitted the most. They gained much more in oil revenues than they lost because of increases in the prices they paid for imports, or because of a narrowing of markets for exports other than oil because of the recession.

In fact, the big influx of income and gold-and-currency reserves to the oil-exporting countries expresses a redistribution of the surplus value produced by the world proletariat, including the proletariat of the semicolonial oil-exporting countries, in favor of the ruling classes of the oil-exporting countries and at the expense of the imperialist bourgeoisies. This redistribution (the appearance of a high mining rent appropriated to a large extent by the local ruling classes) is a result of the economic disproportions underlined above and of a political shift in the relationship of forces on a world scale.

Imperialism was forced to switch from direct to indirect rule over its former colonies after World War II because the anti-imperialist liberation movement became too strong and could not be defeated militarily on a worldwide scale. The imperialist powers tried first to transform the ruling classes in the colonies into junior partners without payment of a substantial economic price for this changed form of rule. Today, through the oil crisis, the bill is being presented by history. Some junior partners are able to demand and obtain a significantly increased portion of the spoils.

While the world balance of forces does not favor an imperialist attack on the Middle East, and while U.S. imperialism favors higher world oil prices to a much larger degree than it publicly pretends, no imperialism favors even the partial redistribution of its wealth to subalterns. The danger of renewed war in the Middle East is consequently very real, especially because of the explosive relations between the Palestinian liberation struggle, the Arab regimes, and Israel.

While the oil-exporting countries will generally strengthen their economic growth, including capitalist industrialization to a limited extent, for the other semicolonial countries the combination of a world recession with sharp increases in the prices of oil, food, and fertilizer has become a major economic disaster—the greatest to hit any part of the world since World War II. The countries of the Indian subcontinent have been hit hardest of all. The increased food, fertilizer, and oil bills; the decrease in their own exports as a result of their inability to compete with the imperialist powers in a period of intensified trade warfare; the decline of their own industrial production triggered by all these developments, which in turn leads to serious difficulties in buying the raw materials necessary for normal industrial production; the ruthless profiteering and hoarding of food reserves by the indigenous ruling classes; the collapse of the "green revolution" as a result of the steep increase in fertilizer and energy costs—all these factors have brought about an explosive increase in misery, underemployment, and outright starvation both in the country-side and the towns.

The ingredients for a social explosion have thus been assembled. But the crisis of proletarian leadership, which is nowhere near its solution, has increased the danger that reactionary right-wing forces will take the initiative in turning the crisis to account at the expense of the masses, who will pay for it in blood and starvation.

10. The noncapitalist character of the economies of the bureaucratized workers' states has been strikingly confirmed—contrary to all the mystifications of the supporters of the theory of "state capitalism"—by the fact that they have not been caught up in the vortex of mass unemployment and decline in production engulfing all the major capitalist countries. On the other hand, those who stick to the parallel mystification of "socialism in one country" will encounter new difficulties in trying to explain why these supposedly "socialist" countries cannot completely cut their ties with the world market, thereby remaining subject to the effects of the world capitalist recession.

These effects can be summarized in four points:

(a) The world recession reduces the export markets of the bureaucratized workers' states in the capitalist countries (except oil, grain, sugar), export markets which these economies urgently need in order to increase their imports of modern equipment. The bureaucracy will try to compensate for this relative decline in its export markets by stepping up the search for loans, in return for which it will be all the more willing to pay the political price of not exploiting the mounting social crisis in the West. The bureaucracy has gone out of its way in giving assurances that it is not going to seek to turn the recession into a revolutionary crisis and that it will see to it that the Communist parties do their utmost to keep the workers within the bounds of class-collaborationist reformism.

(b) The shortage of oil and grain upsets some of the economic plans of the workers' states, especially the heavy importers of these commodities like the German Democratic Republic (GDR) and Cuba. In these instances it could cause a slowdown of the rate of economic growth, especially in combination with a decline of exports to the West.

(c) The shortage of oil and grain, combined with the effects of the recession, creates new stresses and tensions in the relations between the bureaucracies. To sell oil at world market prices to other workers' states (GDR, Cuba, North Vietnam, Hungary, etc.) becomes so lucrative for exporting bureaucracies like the USSR, Rumania, and China that charges will be leveled of exploitation.

(d) The change in the world economic situation increases interest among the imperialist powers in probing the bureaucratized workers' states both as markets for exported goods and as sources of raw materials. The tendency will mount to seek big trade deals like those already made to exchange oil and natural gas of the USSR and China for pipelines, petrochemical plants, petroleum refineries, and other equipment. However, quantitatively, this is not large enough to offset the results of the deceleration in the growth of the volume of world trade which is occurring. Moreover, the deals are of such a long-term character that their effect will be felt only over a period of years.

11. In view of the general increase in social and political contradictions and tensions as a result of the worldwide recession, imperialism will be increasingly tempted to block social explosions by local wars, and to "absorb" some of the major effects of the long-term decline in the rate of growth by stepping up the armaments race. In spite of the policy of détente and peaceful coexistence pursued with complete sincerity by the Stalinist bureaucracies, there are areas in the world where, for obvious reasons, i.e., self-defense, the bureaucracies cannot retreat indefinitely without endangering their own security. Factions prepared to adopt a policy of unlimited retreat in the face of renewed imperialist aggression in those areas would probably meet stiff opposition, in the first place from the army commands.

The Middle East obviously is such a key area of potential conflict today. The economic recession spreading throughout the international capitalist economy, combined with the steep increase in oil prices, has created a dangerous climate of imperialist aggression, politically and economically, in this area. This is the first time since the 1949 recession that a serious downturn in the economic situation of imperialism has coincided with a sharp increase in international tension in an area where a direct military confrontation between imperialism and the armies of the Warsaw Pact is possible.

Up to a certain point U.S. imperialism can carry on maneuvers, horsetrading, and military blackmail with both the Arab ruling classes and the Zionist leaders with the aim of imposing a "settlement" in the Middle East, essentially at the expense of the liberation struggle of the Palestinian masses. The objective of retaining essential control over Middle East oil is to be accomplished through joint ventures with the Arab ruling classes, including massive investments of petrodollars in Western property, the better to tie the Arab rulers to the "economic order" of international capitalism.

The Zionist leaders are not simply puppets of imperialism; they have their own independent interests to defend. Seeing that time works against them, that the relationship of forces in the Middle East could become more and more adverse to the maintenance of an expansionist colonial settler state in the area, they could be tempted to exploit a temporary military superiority at a given moment and undertake a preemptive strike against the neighboring Arab countries. In case of partial failure or in face of heavy retaliation, they might resort to extreme measures, including the use of atomic weapons. This could lead to incalculable consequences through involvement of the world's two major nuclear powers.

The fact that the international working class and toiling masses, including those in the United States, are strongly opposed to warlike adventures is a deterrent to such desperate adventures by the capitalist class. While not underestimating the dangers of a "brush-fire" war in the Middle East, it is unlikely that imperialism will seek a military showdown with the bureaucratized workers' states as long as the international working class has not suffered a disastrous defeat.

Nevertheless, the graver the economic difficulties of world capitalism become, the more the social and political tensions increase, the more will certain sections of the capitalist class tend to intensify war preparations and play with military adventures. Either the danger of war will intensify and along with it the danger of forms of the "strong state" and anti-working-class dictatorships coming to power, or the proletariat will impose its own solution for ending the death agony of capitalism—the conquest of power by the toiling masses, the victory of the socialist revolution.

Bibliography

"What should I read to understand Marxist economics?" The question is often asked and is easy to answer: *Capital,* by Karl Marx, especially the first volume. But everyone who has enthusiastically plunged into that work knows how rapidly we get bogged down in its deep complexities. In fact, it is necessary to read *towards* this book, to read a number of other works first in order to familiarize oneself with the concepts. The following books, all in print, provide a background for understanding Marxist economics. They are listed in a suggested reading order, roughly corresponding to their difficulty, but also alternating between basic theoretical works and analyses of contemporary society.

Mandel, Ernest. *An Introduction to Marxist Economic Theory.* 2nd ed. New York: Pathfinder Press, 1973.

Marx, Karl. *Wage-Labor and Capital.* New York: International Publishers, 1933.

Lenin, V. I. *Imperialism: The Highest Stage of Capitalism.* New York: International Publishers, 1939.

Baran, Paul A., and Sweezy, Paul M. *Monopoly Capital.* New York: Monthly Review Press, 1966.

Braverman, Harry. *Labor and Monopoly Capital.* New York: Monthly Review Press, 1974.

Marx, Karl. *Value, Price and Profit.* New York: International Publishers, 1935.

Engels, Frederick. *Anti-Dühring* (part II). Moscow: Foreign Languages Publishing House, 1954.

Mandel, Ernest. *Marxist Economic Theory.* 2 vols. New York: Monthly Review Press, 1968.

Magdoff, Harry. *The Age of Imperialism.* New York: Monthly Review Press, 1966.

Mandel, Ernest. *The Formation of the Economic Thought of Karl Marx.* New York: Monthly Review Press, 1971.

Marx, Karl. *Capital.* 3 vols. New York: International Publishers, 1967.

Luxemburg, Rosa. *The Accumulation of Capital.* New York: Monthly Review Press, 1968.

Perhaps the best of all guides to Marx's *Capital,* long out of print, was written by an American businessman named William Blake: *Elements of Marxian Economic Theory and its Criticism.* New York: Cordon Company, 1939.

Other Works Cited

Energy Project of the Ford Foundation. *A Time to Choose: America's Energy Future.* Cambridge, Mass.: Ballinger Publishing, 1974.

Heilbroner, Robert L. *The Worldly Philosophers.* 3rd ed. New York: Simon and Schuster, 1969.

Howell, Leon, and Morrow, Michael. *Asia, Oil Politics, and the Energy Crisis.* In *IDOC* (International Documentation) nos. 60–61. New York: IDOC/North America, 1974.

International Institute for Strategic Studies. *Strategic Survey 1973.* London, 1974.

Johnson, Brian. *The Politics of Money.* New York: McGraw-Hill, 1970.

Keynes, John Maynard. *The General Theory of Employment, Interest, and Money.* New York: Harcourt, Brace & World, 1964.

Kindleberger, Charles P. *The World in Depression, 1929–1939.* Berkeley and Los Angeles: University of California Press, 1973.

Kondratieff, Nikolai D. "The Long Waves in Economic Life." In *The Review of Economic Statistics,* vol. 17, no. 6 (November 1935).

Perkins, Dexter, and Van Deusen, Glyndon G. *The United States of America: A History.* New York: Macmillan, 1962.

Preis, Art. *Labor's Giant Step.* 2nd ed. New York: Pathfinder Press, 1972.

Shannon, David A. *The Great Depression.* Englewood Cliffs, N. J.: Prentice-Hall, 1960.

Shuman, James B., and Rosenau, David. *The Kondratieff Wave: The Future of America Until 1984 and Beyond.* New York: World Publishing, 1972.

Trotsky, Leon. *Europe and America: Two Speeches on Imperialism.* New York: Pathfinder Press, 1971.

Trotsky, Leon. *Marxism in Our Time.* New York: Pathfinder Press, 1970.

Trotsky, Leon. "The Curve of Capitalist Development." In *Problems of Everyday Life and Other Writings on Culture and Science.* New York: Monad Press, 1973.

U.S. Bureau of Mines. *Minerals in the World Economy.* Pamphlet preprint from 1971 *Bureau of Mines Minerals Yearbook.* Washington: U.S. Department of the Interior, 1971.

U.S. Senate. *The International Financial Crisis.* Hearings before the Subcommittee on International Finance and Resources, U.S. Senate, 93rd Congress, first session. Washington: U.S. Government Printing Office, 1973.